Anger Management for Everyone

SECOND EDITION

10 Proven Strategies
to Help You Control Anger
and Live a Happier Life

RAYMOND CHIP TAFRATE, PhD
HOWARD KASSINOVE, PhD, ABPP

Impact Publishers, Inc.

Publisher's Note

This publication is designed to provide accurate and authoritative information in regard to the subject matter covered. It is sold with the understanding that the publisher is not engaged in rendering psychological, financial, legal, or other professional services. If expert assistance or counseling is needed, the services of a competent professional should be sought.

Distributed in Canada by Raincoast Books

Copyright © 2019 by Raymond Chip Tafrate and Howard Kassinove
Impact Publishers
An imprint of New Harbinger Publications, Inc.
5674 Shattuck Avenue
Oakland, CA 94609
www.newharbinger.com

Cover design by Amy Shoup

Acquired by Tesilya Hanauer

Edited by Xavier Callahan

All Rights Reserved

FSC
www.fsc.org
MIX
Paper from
responsible sources
FSC® C011935

RAINFOREST ALLIANCE
CERTIFIED

Library of Congress Cataloging-in-Publication Data

Names: Tafrate, Raymond Chip, author. | Kassinove, Howard, author.
Title: Anger management for everyone : ten proven strategies to help you control anger and
     live a happier life / Raymond Chip Tafrate, Howard Kassinove ; foreword by Matthew
     McKay.
Description: Second Edition. | Oakland, CA : Impact, 2019. | Revised edition of the
     authors' Anger management for everyone, c2009. | Includes bibliographical references.
Identifiers: LCCN 2018049382 (print) | LCCN 2018050497 (ebook) | ISBN
     9781684032273 (PDF e-book) | ISBN 9781684032280 (ePub) | ISBN 9781684032266
     (paperback)
Subjects: LCSH: Anger. | Conflict management. | BISAC: SELF-HELP / Anger
     Management (see also FAMILY & RELATIONSHIPS / Anger). | FAMILY &
     RELATIONSHIPS / Anger (see also SELF-HELP / Anger Management). |
     PSYCHOLOGY / Emotions.
Classification: LCC BF575.A5 (ebook) | LCC BF575.A5 T35 2019 (print) | DDC
     152.4/7--dc23
LC record available at https://lccn.loc.gov/2018049382

20   19   18

10   9   8   7   6   5   4   3   2   1   First Printing

Contents

PART 5: Changing Anger Expression

Foreword

An estimated one in five Americans has an anger problem. Anger has enormous costs—for the individual and our society. For the individual who struggles with anger there are often serious health, career, and relationship outcomes. Medical research has implicated anger in disorders such as hypertension, cardio-vascular disease, ulcerative colitis, and increases in all-cause mortality. Anger leads to less satisfaction at work, and, in the words of anger researcher Myer Friedman, "is responsible for repeated disasters—careers wrecked, whole businesses and large enterprises threatened with ruin." In our relationships, anger can be a destructive force that leads to higher divorce rates, broken friendships and family bonds, increased isolation and loneliness, and reduced community and social support.

A large proportion of the physical and emotional abuse suffered by children in our society is driven by chronically angry parents and caregivers. These children often struggle with depression, social alienation, aggressive behavior, delinquency, poor school performance, and poorer overall adjustment. As adults, these victims of angry caregivers have higher rates of depression, relationship dysfunction, emptiness, eating disorders, spouse abuse, and violent crime.

Anger Management for Everyone (2nd Edition) offers effective, comprehensive, and evidence-based solutions to the high personal and social costs of anger. In addition to classic CBT tools such as relaxation, mindfulness, cognitive restructuring, and assertiveness training, Drs. Tafrate and Kassinove offer new response delay techniques, new interventions to address problems with social (as opposed to anger-based) solutions, cutting edge strategies to disarm and avoid provocations, and special techniques to let go and forgive.

Among the foremost anger researchers in America, the authors know the key to successful anger management: *Anger coping skills must be learned while a person is angry.* Research on state-dependent learning has shown us that skills learned in a calm state (while reading this book, for example) often can't be remembered or utilized in an activated (angry) state. That's why anger exposure—visualizing recent upsets and provocations while coping with distress and urges to attack—is essential to changing anger behavior.

At the heart of this book is the SMART program–which stands for Selection Menu for Anger Reduction Treatment. The SMART menu provides multiple options for responding to provocations. Readers will learn to immediately select strategies that are proven to work for them and are appropriate for the triggering situation. The SMART program trains readers to respond quickly and flexibly to anger triggers, and it makes *Anger Management for Everyone (2nd Edition)* the best of all anger self-help titles available today. The skills presented here will change both the frequency and intensity of anger and anger expression. They will change lives.

—Matthew McKay, PhD
Co-author of *When Anger Hurts*

Preface and Acknowledgments

In 2002 we published *Anger Management: The Complete Treatment Guidebook for Practitioners* (Impact Publishers). We geared that text to professionals who were working with angry teenagers and adults. The book and its program were well received, and editions were published in Arabic, Korean, Spanish, Chinese, and Russian. Many people sent us letters and emails telling us how useful they had found the program.

At the same time, we were aware that most people don't go to a professional for help with their anger issues. Therefore, in 2009 we published *Anger Management for Everyone: Seven Proven Ways to Control Anger and Live a Happier Life* (Impact Publishers), and we directed it to people who were interested in learning on their own and helping themselves. That book was also very successful.

But new findings and ideas have emerged since that time, and we have learned even more about how to reduce anger, conflict, and aggression. As a result, we decided to share our updated and expanded knowledge in this volume, the second edition of *Anger Management for Everyone*. All the chapters have been updated, new chapters have been added, and we've incorporated a variety of material—including tips for lifestyle management, information about mindfulness and meditation, thoughts on how words are (or are not) related to reality, and guidance for improving social and interpersonal skills—that, in this edition, adds up to ten strategies for reaching the goal of reducing maladaptive anger. In addition, for the first time, all the practice exercises, along with a host of other materials, are available for download at the website for this book, http://www.newharbinger.com/42266 (see the very back of the book for more details).

We continue to recognize the important work of our many colleagues who have made significant contributions to the study of anger. They have added to our understanding, created techniques for minimizing excessive reactions, and pioneered the development of positive life skills for happiness. Most of the book's chapters don't include formal citations of scientific research, but we've alluded to our colleagues' work by providing a list of selected references and keying them to particular chapters. We've also provided additional resources in the book's two appendices.

Some special people deserve recognition. We thank our many clients, patients, and students, who have shared their personal anger experiences with us. Our knowledge and growth as professionals have improved as we've traveled with them through their personal journeys and conflicts. We also thank Jerry Deffenbacher, Thomas DiBlasi, Raymond DiGiuseppe, Christopher Eckhardt, Albert Ellis, Jeffrey Froh, Damon Mitchell, Raymond Novaco, Denis Sukhodolsky, and Joseph Wolpe, all colleagues who have shaped not just our ideas but the entire field of anger management.

In the production of the first edition, we were very fortunate to work with Dr. Robert Alberti, a leader in the field of assertiveness training. In the production of this edition, we were equally fortunate to work with Dr. Matthew McKay, Xavier Callahan, Tesilya Hanauer, and Caleb Beckwith, who provided much thoughtful guidance and, we think, many improvements.

We are also grateful to our academic institutions for supporting our study of anger-related issues.

Finally, we continue to appreciate the support and love of our wives, Lauren Tafrate and Tina Kassinove, who have helped us live our own lives with minimal anger and maximum happiness.

—Raymond Chip Tafrate
Central Connecticut State University

—Howard Kassinove
Hofstra University

Introduction

What ticks you off? Is it your teenage son who doesn't listen to your advice? How about your life partner who has a roving eye and sometimes doesn't come home when expected? Maybe your employer doesn't appreciate all the honest hard work you do. Or perhaps your mother or father always seems to be picking on you—parents can really drive you crazy, right?

And what about all those stupid drivers? They poke along in the fast lane, tailgate you, and cut you off. They certainly deserve to be taught a lesson! You can honk at them, glare them down, cut in front of them, and teach them to show you some respect. You can also yell at your children, mother, or husband. Or you can get really pissed off and tell your boss you're done. After all, it's time those people learned you aren't going to take it anymore. At the very least, you may think it's important to show your anger and not let others bully you.

You may be thinking about your anger, or the anger of others, because you think it's time to do something about it. Or a friend or a professional you're working with may have suggested this book to you. In any case, there's a good chance that your anger is something you can't ignore any longer. Your angry behavior may be scaring the people you loudly put down, make demands of, or threaten with bodily gestures. And if you're looking honestly at yourself, you may be alarmed when you think about your own excessive reactions, and about where your anger is likely to lead you next.

How does anger show itself in your life? Since you're reading this book, you've probably thought a lot about that question. Will your life really be better if you keep acting out of anger? Actually, as we'll show you in the chapters to come, continuing to act out of anger is likely to make your life worse.

Frank, a thirty-six-year-old long-haul trucker, was often out of town for up to two weeks at a time. Divorced from his first wife, he had been dating Amy for six months and thought they had agreed to stop seeing other people. Frank was even thinking about proposing to Amy.

One evening, after a five-day haul, he drove to Amy's house and saw an unfamiliar car in the driveway. Naturally suspicious, he sneaked up to the bedroom window and saw Amy having sex with another man.

> *Enraged, Frank went to a local bar for a drink. Then he went home and got his shotgun. And then he went back to Amy's and killed her as well as the man she was with. The whole episode took less than an hour. As an outcome, Frank is in prison for the rest of his life.*

Even if you're not as enraged as Frank, your anger may have reached the point where you or your loved ones are becoming concerned. And even if your anger seems to help you feel alive and passionate and energizes you to face problems, it may also lead you into impulsive and even aggressive and destructive acts. Your anger may make it hard for you to think clearly, reach good decisions, and maintain healthy relationships as others become uncomfortable with your behavior and withdraw. Indeed, you may already be painfully aware of what your anger is costing you.

What you'll learn from this book is that frustration, misfortune, unfairness, and disappointment are circumstances that occur in everyone's life, but they do not have to lead to anger or aggression. We'll show you how to think constructively about such circumstances and how to respond to them constructively as well.

Overview of the Contents

The subtitle of this book mentions proven strategies for controlling anger. But in the world of behavioral science, as in every other realm of science, very little is actually proven. Rather, knowledge builds up over time as scientists learn more and more about behavior, including angry behavior. In the spirit of good science, then, this second edition of *Anger Management for Everyone* presents lots of new information along with three additional strategies beyond the seven offered in the first edition. Although most of the chapters don't formally cite scientific studies, the book is grounded in our experience and in high-quality research, our own as well as that of other researchers in the fields of counseling, psychotherapy, and cognitive behavior therapy (CBT). In fact, we think CBT has produced the most advanced and scientifically supported techniques to help people improve their lives, and we lean on CBT a lot.

That said, this book—divided into six parts, with four chapters (4, 8, 10, and 12) new to this edition, and two bonus chapters (14 and 15) available exclusively online and downloadable along with practice exercises—is about putting anger in its proper place so you can live a vital, happy, upbeat life. As you work through the chapters and exercises, learning to reduce your anger, you'll become better able to make good life decisions, improve your relationships, and behave in ways likely to bring about the results you want the most.

Part 1, "Anger Basics" (chapters 1, 2, and 3), contains information intended to help you understand your anger and prepare to change. In chapter 1, we answer some common questions about anger. In chapter 2, we guide you through a process for becoming a keen observer of the details of your own angry reactions (this process is known as an *anger episode analysis*). In chapter 3, we ask you to look at your own arguments for (and against) reducing your anger.

Part 2, "Changing Anger Triggers" (chapters 4, 5, and 6), presents the first three of this book's ten strategies for bringing your anger under control. Chapter 4 offers help with managing aspects of your lifestyle. Chapter 5 shows you both how to change situations that trigger your anger and how to sidestep difficulties by changing the way in which you relate to those triggering situations. In chapter 6, we explore ways of finding solutions to problems in contexts that range from marriage and parenthood to work and traffic jams.

Part 3, "Changing Thoughts That Lead to Anger" (chapters 7, 8, and 9), will help you learn to think differently about negative life events (chapter 7) and figure out how to let go of anger toward those who have mistreated you (chapters 8 and 9).

Part 4, "Changing Internal Anger Experiences" (chapters 10 and 11), discusses the role that relaxation and a meditative state of mind can play in helping you calm your anger (chapter 10) and how deliberate and repeated exposure to anger-provoking situations may be some of the best medicine for maladaptive anger.

Part 5, "Changing Anger Expression" (chapters 12 and 13), teaches you strategies for improving your social and interpersonal skills (chapter 12) and expressing yourself in a more effective, assertive way.

Part 6, "Other Issues" (chapters 14 and 15), focuses on options to consider if anger continues to be a problem for you (chapter 14), and on how to use strategies from the field of positive psychology to live a more vibrant, joyful life (chapter 15). These two chapters can be downloaded from http://www.newharbinger.com/42266, where all the book's practice exercises can also be found.

The book's two appendices list programs helpful in managing problems that commonly overlap with anger (appendix A) and resources for finding qualified therapists in different geographic locations (appendix B).

Getting SMART

Throughout the book, we present stories based on our experiences with clients, patients, colleagues, and research participants, to show you our ten strategies in action with many kinds of anger—between friends and family members, in the workplace or at school, between parents and children, in dating relationships, in traffic, and in decisions about whether to get a divorce. Naturally, we've changed names and other identifying details to respect the privacy and ensure the anonymity of the real people whose stories we've shared.

What the book offers is our Selection Menu for Anger Reduction Treatment (SMART). This means not only that our program is smart but also that you can decide for yourself what you will choose and what you will use, in the same way you would make selections from a restaurant menu. We all have our preferences, and our "choose and use" approach gives you the freedom to explore and work with any and all of the strategies you believe are most likely to help you. We emphasize this approach because it's respectful of the fact that your anger exists in the unique context of your life and is something that only you can deal with.

Our program will teach you how to control the flame of your anger. You'll also learn how to express your anger assertively, and how to seek a constructive dialogue, so you can have fewer arguments with others. And for those times when it's impossible for you to express your anger or have a dialogue, we'll teach you how to relax, accept, forgive, dampen the flame, and move forward with your life.

Getting the Most from This Book

We are here only to guide you in your quest for a calmer and happier life. Our ten strategies for reducing anger are powerful—but no one can force you to use them. We simply hope you will consider the strategies you believe will be helpful to you and then take them for a test drive. In practical terms, this means we will help you *see* new strategies for thinking and behaving, ask you to *try* them, and encourage you to *practice* your new skills often. This formula—*see, try, practice*—is one of the best ways for you to make quick improvements. So read the whole book, understand the program, and select the strategies you want to use. Here are some more tips for getting the most out of reading this book:

- *Take your time.* This isn't a book to be read through in one sitting. It's best to tackle one chapter at a time.

- *Be open.* Some of the information we present may go against ideas you've held for years. Unfortunately, there's a lot of confusion about anger. We hope you'll be open-minded about our recommendations.

- *Download and complete the practice exercises.* Give them your best effort. Just reading about the strategies will not be enough for you to learn to control your anger.

- *Try to transfer your new skills to situations in your life.* Repetition and lots of practice will make new ways of thinking and behaving more comfortable for you, and more automatic.

- *Feel free to pick and choose.* If you try a strategy and it's not a good fit for a specific situation in your life, don't worry—just move on to the next one.

It's important to recognize that a self-help book can't substitute for a complete psychotherapy program. We hope you're not as angry as Frank, who ended two lives and wrecked his own in a single episode of anger. But if anger is still a problem for you after you've given our program a real chance, professional help may be warranted. Either way, whether you're working with a therapist or on your own, the good news is that you *can* learn to reduce your anger and modify your reactions to becoming angry. And as you choose, use, and master our strategies for reducing your anger, you will open the door to greater happiness and a more fulfilling life.

PART 1

Anger Basics

CHAPTER 1

Common Anger Questions and Answers

It is no way of earning people's goodwill by being ill-tempered.

—Baltasar Gracián

Anger can be really nasty. You may have firsthand experience with the pain and suffering it produces. Its toxic effects cut across many areas of life. Anger can ruin relationships. It can increase the risk of heart attacks. And having a life filled with anger is just plain unpleasant.

You may not be sure that you can change the way you act when you're angry. But we think you can, and we applaud you for picking up this book and examining the role that anger plays in your life. That's a big step toward living a more peaceful and productive life.

It's very common for people to react strongly when they're angry. People of all ages, education levels, ethnic backgrounds, and income categories do it. Throughout this book, we present stories of people who have struggled with anger in a wide range of situations. What all the stories have in common is that anger got in the way of the ability to deal effectively with life's challenges. The purpose of this chapter is to answer some basic questions about anger, provide accurate information, and present a base of knowledge that you can draw on as you move forward with your goal of improving your behavior when you're angry. We'll help you make sense of the many parts of anger, and we'll answer common questions about it. And at some point, you'll have to ask yourself this basic question: "Is my anger helpful?"

Understanding Anger

Anger can be difficult to understand. In fact, you may have felt both happy and unhappy after you expressed anger. For example, you can probably remember plenty of times when your anger seemed justified—almost proper. If you're like most people, you've probably said to yourself, "I have a right to be angry after what she did!" Yet, if you're honest with yourself, you can recognize that there have been times when your anger was too strong, lasted too long, created unnecessary problems, or was just plain foolish. You can probably recall times when your anger led to arguments, headaches, regrets, stupid behavior, and other problems, even when you believed it was appropriate.

Anger is one of our basic feelings. Scholars—including Charles Darwin, a naturalist; Robert Plutchik, an evolutionary psychologist; and Paul Ekman, a professor emeritus of psychology—have written about anger in people in all cultures, and from all parts of the world.[1] Anger is common in families, workplaces, and most relationships. Anger, like other emotions, is woven into the fabric of human existence.

Some aspects of anger are positive. It's part of the ups and downs of relationships and can be a useful signal that something isn't right. Some anger can even improve understanding between people. For example, your voice raised in anger can signal to others that you're talking about something important, and it can lead them to listen more carefully to you. Or anger may motivate you to make changes in your life and even face problems that you've been avoiding. Anger can also lead to zest, excitement, and passion. The plain truth is that we wouldn't want to live in a world without anger. It has its benefits, and so this book isn't about entirely eliminating anger from your life.

But anger can also lead to significant loss and suffering. Damage to relationships with family members, friends, and co-workers is a common consequence of anger. Angry people don't think straight, and they make bad decisions. In addition, long-term anger can entail severe medical problems, such as heart disease and stroke. These are just a few of the reasons to keep your anger under control. We'll give you others as you read on.

Common Questions About Anger

"Why do I get angry?" "Why do others in my life treat me so badly?" "How can I make my life better?" As psychologists, we've worked with many adults and teenagers over the years, and we've noticed that the same questions come up over and over again.

What Is Anger?

Anger is an emotional response that you consciously feel. At its core, anger is an internal awareness of arousal, accompanied by specific thoughts, feelings, and desires. Let's take a closer look at its elements:

- Self-talk

- Images

- Bodily sensations

- Patterns of expression

In chapter 2, we'll return to these elements and assist you in analyzing your own anger patterns.

Self-Talk

Self-talk consists of the words you say to yourself that you don't usually share with others. Self-talk is perfectly normal. We think in words, and we all have a steady stream of dialogue going on inside our heads all day long. When you're angry, you may be saying to yourself statements like these:

- How could that bitch do that to me?

- I hate her.

- He's a real jerk—I'd like to really make him suffer.

- That's so unfair.

- I'm really pissed off!

A father may say to himself, "I can't take these kids anymore. Their behavior is intolerable. They never listen. I'm just infuriated with them. I've gotta get out of here." Or a businesswoman may say to herself, "I'm really angry. My co-workers just don't appreciate what I do for them and how I cover for their errors. I'll show them! I'm not going to fix things anymore, and we'll see what the boss says then."

All types of angry self-talk have elements in common:

- A *description of the feeling*: I feel annoyed [angry, furious…].

- An *exaggerated description of the problem*: This situation is just terrible.

- *Blame:* My boss made me so angry—it's his fault.

- *A belief in one's inability to cope with problems:* I just can't deal with my son anymore—I can't take his laziness.

- *Morally based, judgmental thoughts:* She should have acted properly—good people don't do things like that.

- *A condemning idea:* She's a total jerk, a real piece of scum.

- *Thoughts about revenge:* I'm not going to take it anymore. I'll show her who the real boss is!

Although self-talk is mostly private, sometimes it's shared with others. For example, if an angry person is in a dominant social position and feels justified, as when a parent argues with a child, the angry person's thoughts may be expressed directly when they're screamed out loud. At work, however, someone who has negative thoughts about a nasty supervisor may not express her thoughts directly, for fear of being fired or passed over for a promotion, just as a student may not directly express his angry thoughts about a teacher, for fear of being given a bad grade. In these instances, the angry person is more likely to express his or her anger indirectly, by gossiping with others, for example, than to deal with the problem directly.

Images

People often recall images of an event that led to their anger. In your head, you may imagine your boss giving you a reprimand. You may hear your teenager swear in a disagreement with his brother and then see him storm out to be with his friends. You may see your wife or girlfriend flirting with another person while ignoring you. These images may well occur during the daytime hours as you privately dwell on the problem or talk about it with a friend; however, they can be most vivid when you're alone, especially when you're about to fall asleep. You may also have images and fantasies about how you will get even and enact revenge. For example, you may see yourself telling your neighbor off, winning an argument with your spouse or in-laws, shoving someone, or stealing from your employer. The danger, of course, is that such images can fuel actual aggressive behavior.

Bodily Sensations

When you're angry, you may become aware of such bodily sensations as a knotted stomach, tight shoulders, sweating, or a headache. You may not notice any physical symptoms until later, or you may become aware of your own tight fist or pursed lips at the moment of anger. In this sense, anger is an emotion of *excitement*. You can feel your body becoming energized to take some form of action, such as shouting, breaking something, or resisting the ideas of others.

Patterns of Expression

Figure out if you're generally an "innie" or an "outie" when it comes to expressing your anger. You're an "innie" if you generally boil inside but seem cool on the outside. If you tend to show your anger by yelling, screaming, arguing, and being sarcastic, then you're an "outie."

If you're an "innie," your anger is something you usually keep to yourself. You may believe that you'll suffer negative consequences if you're honest or yell and let others know how you feel. Perhaps, over the years, you have learned always to keep a lid on your anger and never to express it. You may well be like a pressure cooker that has a tight seal so no steam can get out. Michelle's story shows this pattern.

Michelle was a forty-four-year-old assistant principal at an inner-city high school. Well trained, with a PhD in administration, she considered herself a good educator.

Unfortunately, Michelle, who was white, was constantly worried that she would lose her job to a minority educator. Although there was no evidence that this would happen, her concern led her to be overly cautious with her peers and superiors. Michelle never expressed annoyance, disappointment, or anger. On the surface, she was supportive and agreed with everyone, no matter what they said. If she disagreed, Michelle kept quiet. She never took sides.

Internally, however, Michelle spent hours in her office or at home stewing about what she saw as the many shortcomings of the school system. She suffered from frequent headaches and stomach upsets, and she often had difficulty sleeping.

Although she was generally well liked, others saw Michelle as ineffective because she never forcefully expressed her ideas for educational change. As a consequence, Michelle was never promoted to school principal.

In contrast to Michelle, the behavior of someone who is an "outie" can escalate to slamming doors, breaking things, and shoving people. If you're an "outie," you may be aware of the potential negative results of such behavior, but you let others have it anyway. "Outies" sometimes say, "I just don't care what happens. I can't take it anymore. I've just gotta express what I feel." Being an "outie" can lead to significant problems with others, since few of us like to be near people who are so outwardly angry.

Paul, a twenty-six-year-old graduate student, told us that he had been afraid of his father all during childhood. His father had yelled at him and belittled him almost daily. The result was that Paul avoided his father as much as possible. Paul was surprised to learn that most of his fellow students were not afraid of their fathers. Clearly, Paul's father was an "outie."

Andy had started an accounting firm with his old friend Rob. For five years the business prospered, and profits rose. But eventually profits began to level off, and the company's net income dropped significantly, even though new clients were calling for services. In time, this decline led to arguments between Andy and Rob about how many employees to hire and how much time each of the partners was devoting to the business, and finally it caused a break in their friendship.

As the arguments became more intense, with each partner accusing the other of not working hard enough and not living up to his end of the business agreement, Andy, in frustration, decided to spend a quiet weekend at the office to look over the books. He discovered that Rob had been paying a lot to an advertising agency to get more business. He also thought that Rob was paying their employees too much and allowing them to take too much paid time off. Furious, he confronted Rob, and they had a major argument. Andy shouted, slammed books against the office table, and made vague threats. Rob denied any wrongdoing and tried to explain his actions. But Andy turned a deaf ear.

Both men began to devote less time to the business, and their income continued to decrease. In the end, they dissolved the company.

Unfortunately, Andy had no savings to open a new business. After being out of work for three months, he got a lower-paying job at a local trucking company. He became depressed and developed heart problems that required expensive daily medications, and he struggled to pay his bills.

Some people are neither "innies" nor "outies"; rather, they routinely hold their anger in, but at times of great frustration they let it out. If this is how you act, it's important to figure out when you're most likely to squelch your anger and when you're likely to express it. The goal is to express anger appropriately rather than always holding it in or always letting it out.

What Causes Anger?

In truth, there are a lot of different causes of anger. That's why you see experts expressing many different opinions on TV, in newspapers, on the radio, and on the internet.

Let's begin with an explanation that pulls together what is accepted by most professionals who study and treat anger:

Anger is an emotional reaction to the unwanted and often unexpected behavior of others. It develops on the basis of a sensed threat to one's physical well-being, property, personal image, sense of fairness, or reasonable desire for comfort. How people communicate anger depends on where they are, and on whether expressing anger has worked for them in the past.

This rather formal explanation refers first to what we call an *immediate cause*: something bad happens (such as learning that a friend has been gossiping about you), and you immediately respond with anger—you blame the other person for the way *you* act when you're angry. Psychologists call this a *stimulus to response* pattern. The stimulus is the friend's gossiping about you; the response is your anger.

But it turns out that this explanation is too simple. It's also wrong. As you will see in chapter 2, we call the belief behind this explanation *the big mistake*. Here, we'll discuss the following causes of anger:

- Learning

- Thinking

- Human nature

Learning

A lot of your anger comes from habits that you've developed over the years. Although there's always some immediate trigger that gets you going, you've spent a long time learning *when* and *how* to become angry.

Learning often involves what psychologists call *modeling*. This means learning by seeing what happens to other people when they get angry (in other words, learning by example). People tend to copy the actions of others, especially when they believe that those actions produce good results. Learning by modeling can come from watching the angry behavior of parents, of peers, or of characters on TV, in movies, and in video games, to name just a few examples. There are a lot of opportunities to learn about anger in this way. Then you take what you've learned about anger and turn it into rules for yourself, such as "If people disrespect or gossip about me, I'll get furious and yell. That's me, and that's what I do!"

Of course, not all angry behavior comes from observing others. You have your own unique personal experiences and learning history. Your learning history is made up of two parts, which psychologists call *reinforcement* and *punishment*. Although you probably don't think much about it, all of your behavior is followed by consequences.

You tend to repeat behavior that results in a consequence you like. For example, if you yell at your son to clean his room, and he does it, you're more likely to yell at him again the next time you want him to clean his room. Behavior that is *reinforced* in the short term (yelling at your son) becomes a long-term habit.

In contrast, sometimes your behavior is followed by a consequence you don't like. For example, if you angrily tell strangers in a movie theater to be quiet, and they curse at you, a response that leads to a noisy and uncomfortable confrontation, you're less likely to tell strangers to be quiet in the future. Behavior that is *punished* in the short term (telling strangers to be quiet) doesn't become a habit.

Over time, reinforcements and punishments shape your habits powerfully. The way you act now when you're angry has a lot to do with the consequences of your past angry behavior.

Thinking

Certain ways of thinking also cause anger. For example, you may misinterpret or distort what other people do or say. You may exaggerate, making small problems into big deals. Or you may be demanding and inflexible in your views. When angry, you probably believe the following propositions:

- You've been neglected, ignored, or treated unfairly.

- Someone else has acted wrongly.

- The person who angered you could have acted better if he or she had really wanted to.

- The person who angered you should have acted better.

Your beliefs about the behavior of others may or may not be true. There may be times when you've been mistaken about the motives of other people. Maybe the friend who isn't returning your calls or responding to your texts is dealing with personal health problems or those of a family member. The potential date who keeps putting you off may be overwhelmed with work projects. Or maybe your teenage daughter, who is supposed to come home by dinnertime, was late because she stopped at the mall to buy you a birthday present—she wouldn't want to tell you that and spoil the surprise.

If you're like most people, you don't consciously evaluate your thinking about bad treatment at the hands of others. Your thoughts just seem to come automatically. Unfortunately, however, over time your conclusions can become distorted, inaccurate, and exaggerated. In that sense, it's your *thinking* that causes your anger. We'll return to this idea in chapter 7 and show you how to evaluate and change the parts of your thinking that are exaggerated and distorted.

Human Nature

It turns out that anger is part of human nature. Anger can also exist in nonhuman animals, and the reasons for angry and aggressive behavior in other animals are similar to our reasons for such behavior.

Monkeys, for example, show anger when their territory is invaded and when other monkeys try to steal their food or mate with their partners. Other animals do things when they're angry to make themselves look big and strong. These actions include making their bodies look bigger, standing on their hind legs, hissing, growling, biting, kicking, and scratching. Such behavior is like a lot of our own. When animals growl or hiss, it's a signal to keep away. Our shouting is like their growling. When animals stand erect and enlarge themselves, they're saying they're too powerful to mess with. That's similar to our waving a fist or leaning forward in a threatening pose.

Anger comes out when we feel threatened—because it worked for prehistoric humans. At the same time, our similarity to other animals involves only a *tendency* or an urge to act in anger. As humans who are also shaped by thinking, reinforcements, families, schools, and culture, we do have the power to overcome such urges.

What Is Aggression?

Anger and its cousin, aggression, are often confused. Anger is an *emotion* you primarily feel inside. Aggression is *behavior* others can observe.

Aggressive behavior is typically shown against other people and includes throwing things, kicking, shoving, hitting, and bullying. It also includes sneaky, indirect actions, such as scratching someone's car or hiding office supplies from a co-worker you dislike.

Aggressive behavior ranges from relatively minor (a teen who pushes a school friend in annoyance) to serious (assault and murder). When we say that some aggression is minor, we don't mean to say it isn't important to recognize and examine it. Intentionally destructive behavior directed against another person is almost always unacceptable. Nevertheless, different aggressive acts will have different negative consequences. Being hit by a thrown pencil at school is minor in comparison to being punched in the face.

Roscoe's story shows how acting aggressively when angry can lead to problems with the criminal justice system.

Roscoe was a twenty-two-year-old single man who lived in a rough urban area. He had grown up poor, hadn't finished high school, and had served time in jail for such offenses as disorderly conduct and brawling.

Roscoe was unsuccessful in his attempts to find steady construction work. As hard as he tried, most of his jobs usually ended badly because of disagreements with his supervisors or co-workers. On several occasions, his verbal quarrels had escalated into threatening, yelling, and shoving.

Believing that he had dealt with more than his fair share of misfortune and bad treatment from co-workers over the years, Roscoe said he didn't take any crap from anyone. This attitude permeated his life—in addition to his problems with work, most of his dating relationships lasted a few months or less, and he had few close friends.

In spite of his lack of career or social success, Roscoe rarely admitted to feeling sad or worried. He described such emotions as "wimpy" and believed that expressing them would make him look vulnerable. But anger was different. Roscoe said his anger made him feel strong and in control, especially when people didn't treat him the way he liked.

Out of work and money, Roscoe decided to break into a local home. He was caught and given a four-year prison term. In prison, he had an argument with an inmate who had made a nasty remark about Roscoe's pimples and receding hairline. Roscoe immediately became infuriated and hit the man with a chair. As a result, he was sentenced to an additional three years in prison.

Aggression also includes the element of *intent*. In order for you to characterize the behavior of your husband, wife, or child (or of a friend, stranger, or co-worker) as aggressive, the behavior has to have been performed intentionally. We don't usually consider dentists or physical therapists to be aggressive, even though they may cause some temporary pain. Their intent is to help us. The law sees intentional and unintentional crimes as very different. Intentional aggression, as when a murder is planned, is punished much more severely than is unintentional aggression, as when a person is hurt in a car accident. Similarly, a friend's intentional bad behavior is far more significant than his or her accidental behavior. When you're examining the bad behavior of others in your life, you'd be wise to consider whether their actions were intentional or not.

Does Anger Cause Aggression?

Sometimes anger is the fuel for aggression. More often, however, anger occurs without aggression. And sometimes aggressive acts occur without anger. Hunters, for example, are aggressive—their intent is to kill animals—yet they don't harbor anger against those animals.

Aggression with Anger

If you read the papers, you may think anger and aggression are like con-joined twins. You often read about crimes of passion—an enraged man attacks his girlfriend after an argument, an angry employee assaults a supervisor after not receiving a raise, an angry teenager shoots his teachers or classmates after he's rejected or misunderstood. But these high-profile cases distort the true picture of the relationship between anger and aggression. It's true that some people do have strong connections between their anger and aggression—they think being angry makes it OK to be aggressive. And lots of the aggression we see on the news and hear about is connected to anger, which is what makes anger and aggression look as if they always occur together. But that's actually the exception, not the rule.

The truth is that intentional physical aggression follows anger less than 10 percent of the time. Most of the time, anger occurs alone, and it's the anger alone that's the real problem for most people. This means that 90 percent of the time, anger shows itself only as yelling, arguing, being verbally demeaning, frowning, getting in a bad mood, or pouting—not as aggression. Even when one person threatens another (for example, an irate parent says, "I'm really gonna let you have it!"), aggression typically doesn't follow anger. By this, we mean there are no observable physical actions associated with the yelling and arguing.

Nevertheless, we don't want to downplay the importance of the relationship between anger and aggression. Anger sometimes *is* followed by aggression, as when the arousal and physical excitement of anger is accompanied by thoughts of revenge and harmful actions. Nevertheless, anger is a serious problem in its own right, regardless of whether it is followed by aggression.

Aggression Without Anger

Aggression and harm to other humans can also occur without anger. In one case, for example, a New York teenager thoughtlessly threw a frozen turkey from a freeway overpass onto a passing car, and a driver was severely injured. But the teen hadn't been angry with that driver. In fact, he had no idea that his thoughtless action might have hurt someone. Or sometimes teenagers and adults behave aggressively not out of anger but as part of a plan to steal from others. A purse snatcher may hurt the arm of the victim and push her to the ground during the theft. The perpetrator isn't angry with the victim. The goal is simply to steal her purse.

Is My Anger Normal?

You may wonder if your own pattern of anger is normal. One way to answer this question is to consider whether situations in your life typically improve or get worse after you become angry. Another way to answer this question is to consider the frequency, intensity, and duration of your anger.

- *How often* do you become angry? In a survey we took of adults living in the community, we found that about 25 percent of people became angry one or more times each week. Some of our research subjects reported getting angry almost every day. Becoming angry seemed to go along with a variety of problems, such as a bad self-image, depression, guilt, weaker relationships with friends and family members, headaches and other medical problems, and legal troubles. Another 25 percent of our research subjects reported becoming angry rarely, if ever. These people seemed to live much happier lives, with far fewer personal, medical, and legal problems.[2]

- *How strong* is your anger? The anger we're calling normal involves a mild to moderate intensity of feeling. Obviously, the more intense your anger is, the more likely it is to cause problems for you. Mild annoyance doesn't create serious disruption in the lives of most people.

- *How long* does your anger last? Some people spend days, weeks, or months dwelling on past unfairness and crappy treatment at the hands of others. Remaining angry for long periods interferes with moving on with life, and with experiencing joy and happiness.

Think about some of the times you've been angry. Have you considered whether your anger was too weak, too strong, or just right? Does your anger occur too often? Does it last too long? Although anger can sometimes be a good thing, you have to look carefully at your life and decide if it's helping or hurting you.

Do Men Get Angrier Than Women?

Another common question has to do with differences between men and women. Many people believe that men are more angry and explosive than women. However, anger seems to be an equal opportunity experience, and the reality is that men and women are much more alike than they are different. A few scientists have even found that women become angry more often than men. For example, John Archer concludes from a large-scale review of scientific studies that women are slightly more likely than men to become angry and to use physical aggression.[3] Of course, since men generally are stronger, when they aggress against women, they produce more harm.

In our professional experience, there's a lot of anger in both men and women. Both sexes seem to become angry with almost equal frequency, for the same reasons, and they experience and express themselves in similar ways. So whether you're a woman or a man, you're definitely not alone. (And keep in mind that the strategies and skills we'll present in chapters 4 through 13 work equally well for both genders.)

Let Anger Out or Hold Anger In?

People often ask us if it's better to hold anger in or let it out. That's the wrong question—both approaches can be bad. It's unwise to hold anger in for long periods of time, and it's unwise to express it impulsively and strongly. Rather, the goal is to minimize anger and express it thoughtfully, in a way that's likely to lead to the resolution of problems.

Does Anger Make Other Problems Worse?

Excessive anger does lead to a range of emotional, behavioral, and medical problems. The most common ones are anxiety, depression, trouble within families, misuse of substances such as alcohol or drugs, and heart disease.

You've probably noticed that you're more likely to become angry when you're worried about important life events, such as problems at work or school or with the behavior of your children, other family members, or friends. As your anxiety rises, your anger fuse becomes shorter. You become less able to tolerate minor frustrations or unwanted hassles. You're clearly more vulnerable to becoming angry when you're anxious, experiencing discomfort, or feeling threatened. Similarly, the negative outcomes of your anger often make difficult situations worse. Reacting with anger seldom solves problems and often creates more. In this way, anger and anxiety can become parts of a vicious cycle.

The same is true for the relationship between anger and sadness. You may have noticed that you're more prone to angry reactions when you're feeling blue and down in the dumps. Some people go back and forth between feeling sad and hopeless and reacting angrily to life's challenges. Furthermore, acting in anger can lead to losses, failures, and isolation. An inability to effectively negotiate the problems of life can very well set the stage for depression.

As mentioned earlier, anger often goes along with substance misuse. You may be tempted to take tranquilizers or sleeping pills or drink alcohol to try to relax or calm the tense physical symptoms of anger. But these are habit-forming methods of coping, and dependence on these substances can come quickly. Some folks, unfortunately, resort to street drugs to cope with their anger, behavior that leads to even more problems.

As also mentioned earlier, intense and prolonged anger goes along with a number of serious medical conditions, such as heart disease, stroke, high blood pressure, and perhaps even diabetes. The connection between anger and these types of medical conditions is often overlooked. Over time, however, strong experiences of anger are likely to take a toll on your physical health. These conditions usually don't emerge right away. Instead, they appear after years of anger-related difficulties. Getting a handle on the way you act when you're angry may be more important than you've ever realized!

Changing the Way You Act When You're Angry

It takes thoughtful analysis and practice to change any type of habit, whether it has to do with smoking, drinking, a spending pattern, or how you behave in a relationship. That's one reason why changing your behavior and learning to manage your anger can be hard. Another is that certain short-term benefits—a momentary feeling of being right or in control, the thought that others are now listening to your demands or will now stop criticizing you, even thoughts of revenge—can make it challenging for you to change your reactions. These immediate satisfactions don't just keep your anger going. They make change difficult when they're coupled with your natural tendency to react when you're threatened. Nevertheless, we're confident that, with practice, you can improve the way you act when you're angry, and that you can change for the better.

Key Points

☑ Anger is an emotion—something you primarily feel inside your body—that can energize you to take constructive or destructive action.

☑ Aggression is different from anger. Aggression involves such behavior as hitting, bullying, shoving, and destroying property.

☑ Anger doesn't automatically lead to aggression.

☑ Anger comes from what you have learned (your habits), your ways of thinking, and your human nature.

☑ To figure out if your anger is normal, think about whether your problems get better or worse after you become angry.

☑ Men and women become angry for the same reasons, and they feel and express anger in similar ways.

☑ Your anger is probably not in your best interests if it's frequent, intense, or long-lasting.

☑ Anger is related to anxiety, depression, alcohol and drug use, heart disease, and stroke.

☑ Here is a key question to ask yourself (and answer honestly): "Is my anger helping or hurting me?"

CHAPTER 2

Understanding Your Anger Episodes

As people are walking all the time, in the same spot, a path appears.

—Lu Xun

* If you are like many other people, your anger probably seems to explode without warning, and that makes it difficult to manage. But the truth is that anger is not an isolated, unpredictable explosion. It occurs as part of a chain of events.

All anger episodes follow a predictable pattern. An examination of your own pattern is the first step toward achieving better control. We call this examination an *anger episode analysis*. It will be helpful to look at your anger reactions from this perspective.

Most people believe it's the crummy behavior of others or some other external event that is responsible for their anger. We refer to this belief as *the big mistake*. In reality, anger is caused not only by external events but also by a combination of factors, including these:

- How you evaluate or interpret external events

- Your biological background as a human being

- How you think about a difficulty or a challenge that occurs in your life

* Before you begin this chapter, we recommend that you download practice exercise 2 (Anger Episode Record) from http://www.newhar binger.com/42266.

Chances are also good that you've developed personal patterns of experiencing and expressing anger. These patterns may include thoughts you have or images you see in your head, physical sensations (such as tightening up), and reactions like yelling, throwing something against a wall, or breaking objects. This chapter will help you see your patterns more clearly.

When you come to understand the unique features of your anger episodes, it will be much easier for you to make changes in what have always seemed to be automatic reactions. In addition, an understanding of the components of your anger episodes will help you examine the results of these episodes and clearly see when anger works for you and when it doesn't.

Our model for analyzing an anger episode is simple. It will help you increase your self-awareness and gain a sense of mastery over your anger. Throughout this chapter we'll use the example of Harvey, who was very confused about his own angry reactions, to illustrate the six parts of an anger episode analysis. The best way for you to understand your own anger, of course, is to apply the same analysis to your own recent experiences of anger, using practice exercise 2 to thoroughly examine all the components of one or more of your anger episodes. As you complete multiple records of your anger episodes, you will solidify your understanding of the Anger Episode Analysis Model. That understanding will serve you later on as you read about and spend time on the strategies you think will be on target and helpful for your particular patterns.

Harvey the Furious Boss

Harvey, thirty-nine years old, managed a building-products business that his father had begun fifty years earlier. With great pride, the company sold roofing, siding, and other home products both to the public and to professional contractors. The company was very successful and had plenty of money in the bank. Harvey lived well, as did his senior employees.

Harvey supervised a sales force of twenty people as well as thirty warehouse workers, and he saw himself as a caring boss. When things were going well on the sales floor, Harvey was very pleasant to be around. But when someone made a mistake, an uglier side of Harvey emerged. He would immediately explode, screaming at the wrongdoer in front of the other employees, not to mention his customers.

Sooner or later, Harvey treated almost every one of his employees this way. He never threatened to fire or demote anyone. He just blew up in anger about the mistake and then went to his office to stew. It usually took more than an hour for him to cool down.

When we spoke with Harvey, he said he had been like this all his life.

"My anger just erupts," he said. "I don't understand what happens. It's beyond me."

Harvey had no awareness of the stages he went through when he got angry. His first step toward achieving better control was to become more aware of the individual components of his anger

Anger Episode Analysis

We developed our Anger Episode Analysis Model on the basis of our research into how people experience anger in the real world. Our studies have included subjects from across the United States as well as from South Korea, Russia, Romania, and India.[4] The model represents an episode of anger as consisting of six components:

1. Trigger

2. Thoughts

3. Experience

4. Action urge

5. Anger expression

6. Outcomes

For the sake of clarity, we will describe the *trigger, thoughts,* and *experience* components before moving on to the other three components of an anger episode, since any of these first three components may lead directly to an *action urge* (that is, an immediate impulse), to *anger expression,* and to one or more *outcomes,* whether negative or positive. The following illustration shows the six components of an anger episode and how they are related.

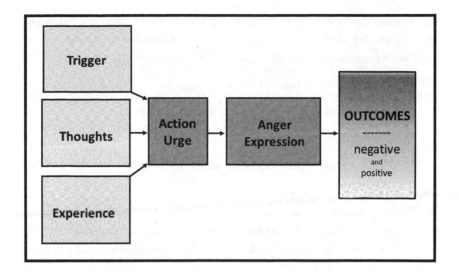

Anger Episode Model (Kassinove and Tafrate, 2019)

Component 1. Trigger

The anger sequence starts with a triggering event. Triggers are usually everyday situations that involve a disagreement, disrespect, a struggle about what to do, a disappointment, or a challenge to ideas or actions. Many times, some kind of stress, threat, unfairness, loss, or potential loss is involved.

People in general become angry about the same kinds of relationships or events. Therefore, if you're struggling with anger, it's likely that you're reacting to the same situations that we all experience from time to time. Nevertheless, your reactions may be more extreme than those of most other people and can lead to worse outcomes. It's important for you to know what triggers your anger, since that information will help you identify the typical starting points in the anger chain that ultimately disrupts your life.

A wide variety of situations, as well as actions by others, can set the stage for anger. Let's review some of the most common triggers.

Others' Negative Behavior

The most common type of anger trigger is an unwanted, unexpected, perceived negative act (or failure to act) by another person who is well known and liked, even loved. This type of trigger includes being ignored, disrespected, and rejected, as when your ideas are criticized or dismissed, or your hard work is taken for granted. Here are some examples:

- He doesn't even listen to my ideas.

- She just wants to do what she wants.

- He didn't support my sales plan.

- After I spent three hours looking for her gift, she said I wasn't thoughtful.

We all occasionally become angry with strangers, but if you review your own anger patterns, you'll probably see that most of your anger arises when you're dealing with people you're close to, such as your children, your parents, your spouse or live-in partner, your co-workers, and your friends.

It's also true that a remark or action that one person would find positive or helpful can trigger another person's anger, especially if the remark or action is unwanted or uninvited:

Susan, an account executive, had a male co-worker who told her almost every day that she was "hot." After the first few times, Susan began to find this supposed compliment offensive, and eventually she became angry.

Liora, a new mother, received a constant stream of unsolicited parenting advice from Ellen, her mother-in-law. Ellen had good intentions, and her advice was often solid. Over time, however, Liora came to experience Ellen's advice as irritating. Liora's irritation led to anger, to quarrels with Ellen, and finally to avoidance of Ellen's company.

Inanimate Objects

Perhaps you've become angry with a computer, a game console, your cell phone, your car, or a copy machine when it stopped working properly. People sometimes scream at, punch, or throw the objects they're mad at. Most people, of course, feel foolish after they've expressed anger at an object. For some people, however, destroying expensive property in a fit of anger becomes a real problem:

Jessica, thirty-four years old, became frustrated with a washing machine in the basement of her apartment building. The machine took only $1 bills, and all she had was a $5 bill. In a fit of anger, she broke the door of the machine, an act that was recorded by the security camera. Jessica's anger cost her $500.

Your Own Behavior

You may experience anger in relation to your own actions. In other words, you may become angry with yourself about something you've done and regretted:

- Trevor, a thirty-two-year-old cashier, said, "I'm so angry at myself for letting him do that to me."

- Clarice, a twenty-seven-year-old single mother, said, "I'm pissed at myself for not saying something to her."

If your anger is directed at yourself, it's likely that you also experience additional emotions when you're angry, such as guilt, shame, and sadness.

Extreme Circumstances

Some anger develops from traumatic events, such as a physical or sexual assault, a robbery, a crippling illness, the unexpected death of a loved one because of apparently incompetent medical care, or a natural disaster like a hurricane or a fire. Life is unpredictable, and everyone is vulnerable to such experiences, but extreme life events can lead to long-term, enduring anger, with fantasies of revenge:

Jeong-Ho was a twenty-four-year-old graduate student in sociology. As a child in South Korea, he had been sexually abused by his middle school teacher. Now, almost twelve years later, Jeong-Ho lived in the United States, far away from the abuser. Jeong-Ho was a successful student, with many friends, but he continued to ruminate about the past mistreatment and had dreams about getting even with the abusive teacher.

As you'll see in later chapters, remaining angry isn't the only option for dealing with extreme circumstances. Indeed, bitterness contributes nothing at all to mental health and well-being.

Memories

Anger can also be triggered when you have a memory of being abused, neglected, or treated unfairly. Memories of mistreatment can take on a life of their own and become obsessive. Such memories may involve the recent past or a time as remote as early childhood. They can evoke relatively minor mistreatment (a parent's favoritism, for example) or more extreme, life-altering circumstances (for example, a physical assault).

Harvey's Trigger: *An Employee's Error*

The building products sold by Harvey's company were priced at a 20 percent discount for contractors, who then installed the products for homeowners, and the homeowners in turn paid the contractors the retail price. Retail customers were also free to purchase products on their own, paying full price.

When one of Harvey's employees made an error, it usually had to do with pricing and delivery dates. For example, from time to time a salesperson would mistakenly charge a retail customer the wholesale price, or salespeople sometimes promised to deliver goods that weren't in stock.

It was this second type of error that had triggered the anger episode Harvey chose to examine with the Anger Episode Record (see fig. 2.1). Not for the first time, Maria, a member of the sales staff, had promised a customer some roof shingles that were out of stock, and she had said they would be delivered in three days. When Harvey heard about the error, and when he recalled that Maria had previously made false promises to customers, he angrily confronted Maria.

"How could you make such a stupid mistake?" he screamed. "I don't understand how you could do this! Didn't you check the stock in the warehouse? You've been with us for five years. You should have known better! You've really made a mess. Damn!"

Part 1. Trigger

Place a check mark next to the word indicating the area of your life in which your anger was triggered.

___✓___ Work

_____ School

_____ Family

_____ Parenting

_____ Romantic relationship

_____ Friendship

_____ Other: _____

In one simple sentence, report the event that led to your anger. (Example: "My son forgot again to clean his room.")

For the third time, Maria promised that we would deliver unavailable roofing shingles in three days.

Figure 2.1. Harvey's Responses to Part 1 of Practice Exercise 2

Component 2. Thoughts

Human beings are thinking creatures. We constantly evaluate what's going on in front of us. We also think and plan for the future and reflect on events that have already happened. In order to understand anger, then, we need to know something about the way we think.

To understand the role of your thoughts (that is, your evaluations, judgments, and appraisals) in the chain of events leading to anger, consider the example of teasing. People tease each other all the time—to strengthen relationships, flirt, play with each other, and resolve conflicts and bad feelings. A lot of teasing is done in fun, but being teased can lead you to feel anger, shame, or humiliation if you see it as insulting rather than playful. Whether a playful statement like "Well, aren't you a know-it-all" leads to laughter or anger will depend on how you interpret the statement.

A very bright student named Martin was well liked by his peers and his professors. In jest, he was often called Smarty Marty. Although Martin could have seen this nickname as a put-down, he always took it with good grace and never became angry.

It's not just being called Smarty Marty (or, for that matter, Dopey, Silly, Baldy, Geeky, or Shorty) that creates anger. Anger arises when teasing statements are heard as demeaning and disrespectful. How you judge others' intentions makes all the difference in whether or not you become angry.

Of course, not all thoughts lead to anger. As it turns out, there are some common thoughts that are part of most people's anger experiences. These thinking patterns were first identified by Albert Ellis and Aaron Beck, who developed a successful treatment called *cognitive therapy*.[5] See if you recognize any of the following types of thoughts in your own anger experiences.

Awfulizing

This type of thinking involves exaggeration. Daily hassles are described as awful, horrible, or terrible when in fact they're ordinary and manageable. Awfulizing leads to complaints about how incredibly bad a problem is, and such complaints waste time and effort that could be devoted to productive problem solving. Putting your energy into creating solutions is better than exaggerating and whining about circumstances you don't like. And nobody wants to hang around with someone who endlessly exaggerates and gripes about problems.

Low Frustration Tolerance

People who don't tolerate frustration well are underestimating their ability to deal with misfortune. Adversity, instead of being viewed as a normal part of life or a challenge to be faced, is seen as intolerable.

Of course, there's a relationship between low frustration tolerance and awfulizing. When you think of a situation as awful or catastrophic, you're less likely to believe you can tolerate it. In the end, people who think in this way typically *do* tolerate the situations they complain about, in spite of all their bluster.

Bettina used to say, "I just can't take it when my kids bicker with each other." Nevertheless, she took it for the next ten years, until they went off to college.

John used to say, "My boss treats me horribly. I can't take him anymore." Nevertheless, he stayed on the job for another twenty-one years.

Seymour used to say, "I have so much trouble at home. My wife doesn't keep the house clean. The kids are out of control. My computer is always broken, and my car is ready for the junkyard. I can't stand my life." Nevertheless, he remained with his family for the rest of his life.

What about you? Do you awfulize, moan about misfortune, and believe you aren't capable of handling life's problems? Or do you see your difficulties as interesting challenges to be met?

Demandingness

When you believe that other people *must* act the way you want them to act, you've assumed a posture of *demandingness*. To put this idea another way, demandingness is the elevation of your personal views to the status of absolute rules, and the imposition of these rules on other people as well as on the world around you. Of course, we all sometimes wish that others would behave the way we'd like. We also may want the world to conform to our personal desires. But there's a difference between wanting and demanding different behavior from others. Demandingness shows up when you use terms like "should," "must," "ought to," and "have to."

Are you a demander? Or do you accept the fact that a lot of things in your life won't go the way you'd like?

Rating Others

In this type of thinking, you see the person who instigated your anger in global, negative, extreme terms. You condemn that person's total existence on the basis of a few actions:

- If you have a disagreement with a friend or family member, you may say to yourself, "Who the hell is she to tell me what to do? She's a total moron. I don't want to have anything to do with her."

- If you're inconvenienced by an inconsiderate driver, you may say to yourself, "He should get the hell out of the passing lane. Jerk! What an ass!"

At one time or another, however, most people you love or like will disappoint you. And not only do you have very little information about an inconsiderate driver, if you're honest with yourself, you will also acknowledge that you haven't always been a perfect driver, either. But you probably wouldn't describe yourself in such negative terms for disappointing someone, driving badly, or making a mistake.

Thinking about others in global and extreme terms will surely fuel your anger and make it difficult for you to resolve problems and maintain relationships:

- He's just a…

- She's a total…

- What a jerk!

Does any of that sound like you? Do you totally condemn others even though you know they do good things as well as bad? Or can you separate other people's individual actions from your total ratings of those people?

Rating Yourself

As we've seen, when things don't go well, you may find that your anger is triggered by your own behavior. When that happens, you may criticize yourself harshly and put yourself down:

- I'm a loser.

- I can't do anything right.

- I'll never succeed.

As mentioned earlier, if rating yourself is one of your thought patterns, you probably experience guilt, shame, and sadness along with anger.

Distortion or Misinterpretation

When you're angry, your evaluations of other people's motives and intentions are more likely to be distorted.

Friedrich, thirty-three years old, described his in-laws' frequent phone calls and visits as "totally intrusive." He often felt angry with his in-laws because he believed their calls and visits were motivated by their lack of trust in him and their desire to check up on their daughter. When Friedrich examined the situation more closely, however, he saw that they just enjoyed spending time with their daughter and their grandchildren. The motivations that Friedrich attributed to his in-laws were distortions of their actual intentions.

The tendency to misunderstand the behavior of others or distort what is going on is especially common when situations are ambiguous. How clearly do you assess situations when you're angry? Have there been times when your thoughts about an event were completely off the mark?

Harvey's Thoughts: *Awfulizing, Low Frustration Tolerance, and Demandingness*

After some discussion, Harvey freely admitted that he had a tendency to awfulize about problems at work. He eventually recognized that if a salesperson promised delivery of an out-of-stock item, the problem could be easily fixed if the salesperson called the customer, explained that there would be a delay, and apologized. Harvey also recognized his low frustration tolerance and his tendency to minimize his ability to cope with difficulties. In addition, Harvey was a demander. He wasn't just hoping that his employees wouldn't make mistakes. He thought that their performance should be perfect at all times. But Harvey did not put his employees down in a global way, and he did not belittle himself. Nor had there been any distortion involved in this anger episode, since a member of his sales staff actually had made an inappropriate promise to a customer. Therefore, Harvey placed a check mark next to only three of the items in the "Thoughts" section of his Anger Episode Record (fig. 2.2).

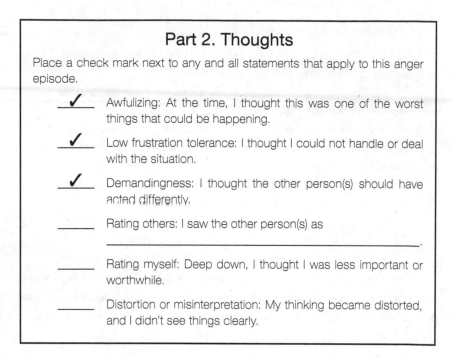

Figure 2.2. Harvey's Responses to Part 2 of Practice Exercise 2

Component 3. Experience

Anger, as defined in chapter 1, is something you feel inside. In our model, the *experience* component has to do with your awareness of three aspects of your anger:

1. How *strong* your anger is (its *intensity*)

2. How *long* your anger lasts (its *duration*)

3. How your anger *feels* physically (the bodily *sensations* of anger)

Intensity

One goal of learning to manage your anger is to become able to express your feelings directly to another person, using words that convey the true nature of your anger. Part 3 of practice exercise 2 (the "Experience" section) allows you to rate the degree of the anger you felt during an anger episode, from 1 (almost no anger) to 10 (extreme anger), and to associate your anger with words that not only convey how intense it was ("mild," "moderate," "strong," and so forth) but also describe how you were feeling ("annoyed," "fired up," "incensed," and so forth). As you familiarize yourself with the use of such words, whether you discover that you're irritated, indignant, or unhinged with rage, you'll develop an emotional vocabulary for more clearly communicating the intensity of your anger to others. Nevertheless, it's also important to understand that the proper expression of anger *never* includes threats of aggression. As a rule, appropriate anger is of mild to moderate intensity, and it can be expressed simply: "I feel...."

Duration

Refer again to part 3 of practice exercise 2 (the "Experience" section). Remember one of your anger episodes, and make your best estimate of how long your anger lasted. Then place a check mark next to the appropriate word ("minutes," "hours," or "days"). If the situation is continuing, and if the anger still exists, place a check mark next to the word "ongoing."

Sensation

People experience a wide variety of physical sensations when they're angry. These include an accelerated heart rate, sweating, muscle tension, a headache, an upset stomach, and shaking. In fact, a rapid heart rate, muscle tension, and trembling are among the most commonly reported physical sensations of anger. Refer again to the "Experience" section of practice exercise 2, and think about each of the physical sensations present during one of your recent episodes of anger. It isn't unusual to experience multiple physical sensations, and so it's OK to place a check mark next to more than one of the words or phrases under the question "What physical sensations did you notice?"

Harvey's Experience: *Intense but Short-Lived Anger*

Harvey had initially felt very strong anger, and he gave it a rating of 8 on his Anger Episode Record (fig. 2.3). Within an hour, however, his anger had diminished. He thought it had mostly dissipated within thirty to forty-five minutes, and so he checked off "minutes" in response to the question about his anger's duration. As for his physical sensations, a discussion helped him highlight having experienced a headache, indigestion, and fuzzy feelings after retreating to his office. These feelings, too, are checked off on Harvey's Anger Episode Record.

Part 3. Experience

Place a check mark next to the number that corresponds to the intensity of your anger, the extent of your anger, and how you felt in this situation.

Intensity of Your Anger	Extent of Your Anger	How You Felt
_____ 1	Almost no anger	Calm, indifferent
_____ 2	Slight anger	Jarred, moved, stirred, ruffled, challenged
_____ 3 _____ 4	Mild anger	Annoyed, bothered, irritated, perturbed, flustered, uneasy, provoked, impelled, cranky, crotchety, distressed, disturbed
_____ 5 _____ 6	Moderate anger	Mad, agitated, pissed off, irked, aggravated, fired up, riled up, all worked up, peeved, indignant
_____ 7 ✓ 8	Strong anger	Irate, inflamed, exasperated, fuming, burned up, incensed, infuriated, enraged, hysterical
_____ 9 _____ 10	Extreme anger	Frenzied, vicious, unhinged, up in arms, rabid, crazed, maniacal, wild, violent, demented

Now complete the following sentence.

At the time of this specific event, I felt *incensed and furious*.

How long did your anger last?

___✓___ Minutes   _____ Days

_____ Hours   _____ Ongoing

What physical sensations did you notice?

_____ Fluttering/upset stomach   _____ Sweating

___✓___ Indigestion   _____ Warmth/flushing

_____ Rapid heart rate   _____ Nausea

_____ Dizziness   _____ Rapid breathing

___✓___ Fuzziness/feelings of   ___✓___ Headache
        unreality
                                           _____ Tingling

_____ Muscle tension
                                           _____ Trembling

_____ Fatigue
                                           _____ Other: _____

Figure 2.3. Harvey's Responses to Part 3 of Practice Exercise 2

Component 4. Action Urge

When you're angry, your urge to take action is complex and determined by multiple factors. As noted earlier, it may come directly from the trigger, from your thoughts, from your internal experience, or from all three of the first three components of the Anger Episode Model.

Like all other animals, you are preprogrammed to react to a perceived threat with anger and aggression. Just try taking food away from a hungry dog, or getting between a mother bear and her cubs! The biological drives for self-preservation and protection of offspring are alive in all of us, and they can urge any animal, including a human being, to get angry and act aggressively. Most of the time, though, human beings face real or perceived threats that are verbal, symbolic, and otherwise far less serious than those faced by animals in the wild. For example, your anger may emerge if you're called a nasty name, or if you discover that others have been gossiping about you. Nevertheless, your primitive, biologically wired urge to take action when you're angry can show itself in retaliatory verbal attacks or behavior. And in our modern world, unfortunately, the urge to take action when we're angry drives behavior that tends to make situations worse.

An action urge has four major characteristics:

1. It emerges as an immediate reaction to a real or perceived threat, before any thinking about the triggering situation even becomes possible.

2. It may be fueled by some of the maladaptive thought patterns we've already discussed, by a strong internal experience, by a bodily sensation, or by all three factors.

3. In some situations, it can lead immediately to impulsive behavior.

4. It some situations, it can be resisted.

Since the urge to action is entwined with the biological history of our species, you have to learn how to delay your response to a nasty trigger so you can evaluate it appropriately before taking action. *And this is something you can learn.* Like other animals, even though you have an urge to act, you may not actually engage in aggressive or retaliatory behavior. Instead, you may just sit and stew, choosing not to give in to the urge and taking another course of action. Remember, an urge can feel quite compelling, but you don't have to act on it.

Harvey's Action Urge: *Using Words as a Weapon*

Harvey felt threatened by his salesperson's error. He perceived it as a danger to his reputation and that of his company. He acted immediately on his urge to unleash a nasty verbal attack, before his employee even had a chance to explain (see fig. 2.4).

Part 4. Action Urge

Place a check mark next to the word(s) or phrase(s) corresponding to your action urge(s) in this situation, and briefly describe the impulse that arose for you. (Examples: "I just wanted to get in his face" or "I couldn't wait to get away from her.")

___✓___   Confront

I wanted to confront and verbally blast her.

_____   Withdraw

_____   Resolve the problem

_____   Other: _____

Figure 2.4. Harvey's Response to Part 4 of Practice Exercise 2

Component 5. Anger Expression

A number of expressive patterns or actions may fit with, or follow, your personal experience of anger. Indeed, people who are angry express themselves in a lot of ways. Here are some of the most common. Do you see any patterns that are similar to yours?

No Expression

Some people tend to keep their anger inside. For example, you may be aware of your anger, but you may also decide that it's too risky for you to show it. Even if you work hard to hide your anger, however, you may still have angry thoughts, and you may brood about the problem that has triggered your anger. If you're holding your anger in, you may be doing so as a result of your passivity and lack of assertiveness. While holding your anger in, you may also be holding long-term grudges, and this behavior may be keeping you from solving your problems.

Indirect Expression

Some people—and maybe you're one of them—express their anger indirectly. This pattern can include a variety of behavior:

- Ruining social or work relationships

- Gossiping or spreading misinformation to harm the targets of your anger

- Passively resisting demands to perform at expected levels in jobs and relationships

- Not following rules

- Not carrying your weight on team projects

- Not responding to requests made by romantic partners or other important people in your life

Outward Verbal Expression

People most commonly express their anger in words, engaging in one or more of the following types of verbal behavior:

- Yelling

- Accusing

- Threatening

- Cursing

- Arguing

- Demanding

- Making nasty remarks

- Using sarcasm

Outward Expression Against an Object or a Person

Physical expressions of anger are less common than verbal expressions but are likely to result in more serious consequences. Here are examples of this type of behavior:

- Hitting

- Kicking

- Shoving

- Throwing or breaking objects

- Slamming doors

- Destroying property

Expression of anger against an object or a person may also be part of a pattern of intimidation and bullying.

Outward Expression Through Bodily Gestures

Here are some common ways to express anger through a bodily movement or gesture:

- Rolling your eyes

- Crossing your arms

- Glaring

- Frowning

- Giving someone the finger

Avoidance

Some people work hard to *not* experience anger. And when anger inevitably arises anyway, despite their best efforts to avoid it, they choose to withdraw from the situation and other people. Watching TV, listening to music, reading a book, and playing a video game are all distractions that can be used to avoid the experience of anger.

Substance Use

Another type of behavior that occurs in connection with angry feelings and thoughts is use of alcohol, prescription drugs, and recreational drugs. As we noted in chapter 1, substance misuse is a problem that very commonly overlaps with anger. Using alcohol or drugs to cope with your anger helps you avoid your problems in the short term, but it's likely to create other difficulties for you in the long run.

Attempts at Resolution

Anger isn't always a bad thing. Sometimes it can help you solve a problem. When people are angry, sometimes they want to cool down and try to come up with a compromise or another kind of resolution. Has anger ever energized you to face a problem or deal with a difficult situation?

Harvey's Anger Expression: *Verbal Attack and Retreat*

Harvey was generally an expresser—an "outie," as discussed in chapter 1. At work, he rarely held his anger in, nor did he express it indirectly, and he didn't avoid situations that triggered his anger. He reacted directly with verbal abuse, though he never got physical by hitting or shoving anyone. He never took medications or used alcohol at work. Sadly for his employees, however, he also never tried to resolve a triggering situation. He would just hole up in his office, allow his anger to diminish of its own accord, and then return to the sales floor and act as if nothing had happened (see fig. 2.5). Naturally, his employees, who bore the brunt of his fury, felt demoralized.

Part 5. Anger Expression

Place a check mark next to any and all behavior you engaged in during this anger episode.

_____   No expression (kept things in, boiled inside, held grudges and didn't tell anyone)

_____   Indirect expression (secretly did something to harm the other person, spread rumors, ignored what the other person wanted)

__✓___   Outward verbal expression (yelled, screamed, argued, threatened; made sarcastic, nasty, or abusive remarks)

_____   Outward expression against an object (broke, threw, slammed, or destroyed an object)

_____   Outward expression against a person (fought, hit, kicked, or shoved someone)

_____   Outward expression through bodily gestures (rolled eyes, crossed arms, glared, frowned, gave a stern look)

__✓___   Avoidance (escaped or walked away from the situation; distracted myself by reading, watching TV, listening to music)

_____   Substance use (drank alcohol; took medications; used other drugs, such as marijuana or cocaine)

_____   Attempt at resolution (compromised, discussed, or came to some agreement with the other person)

_____   Other_____

Figure 2.5. Harvey's Responses to Part 5 of Practice Exercise 2

Component 6. Outcomes

As we've seen, every anger episode results in one or more outcomes, positive or negative. And every outcome of angry behavior helps to determine whether that angry behavior will be repeated in the future.

- If you've found that a type of angry behavior typically has led to a positive outcome (as when you've gained someone's attention, compliance, or admiration), you are likely to repeat that behavior.

- If you've found that a type of angry behavior typically has *not* led to a positive outcome (as when it was ignored, or when you and a friend or partner drifted apart), you are less likely to repeat that behavior.

- If you've found that a type of angry behavior has been punished (as when you've been fired or arrested), you may decide to suppress that behavior.

You can think of your anger episodes as leading to both short-term and long-term outcomes. A short-term outcome appears either during the anger episode or shortly afterward, and it has the greatest likelihood of influencing your angry behavior, since a consequence that is close in time to its cause has the most powerful effect. One possible short-term outcome involves the behavior of other people, as when your wife or husband, child, or employee immediately complies with your angry demands. Another outcome is the release of two chemicals—epinephrine and cortisol—that produce a surge of energy. Your heart rate speeds up, your blood pressure and body temperature rise, your breathing becomes more rapid, you perspire, and your mind becomes sharper and more focused. In a situation where at first you may have felt demeaned and powerless, you now have a feeling of power, thanks to the chemical rush. A strong feeling of anger can also give you the illusion of being capable and in control of a situation in which you've sometimes felt helpless. In this way, the compliant behavior of others, and the chemical reactions that take place within your body, reward your anger in the short term.

A long-term outcome of anger appears after the anger episode has ended. A long-term outcome is generally undesirable, but some long-term outcomes are good. For instance, people have told us that anger makes them successful on the job, and that where they stand on difficult issues is clear to everyone else. A lifetime of being angry does have occasional benefits. But people who have reacted with anger for a long time do tend to experience a lot of bad long-term outcomes. For some people—and you may fit into this category—anger doesn't just energize behavior; it disrupts behavior. For these people, anger doesn't improve communication; it threatens others. For people in this group, anger doesn't just bring a feeling of being more powerful in a difficult situation; it instigates aggressive behavior. Nevertheless, there may be negative outcomes of an anger episode that don't appear for some time. These negative long-term outcomes of anger, like the long-term effects of exposure to toxic chemicals, appear only after years of agitation, argument, and discord. It may even be difficult to understand that these outcomes are linked to anger, since they take so long to emerge. But rest assured—anger is a very real problem over the course of a lifetime. Here is a short list of its long-term negative outcomes:

- Relationship and family conflict

- A poor reputation

- Workplace problems, leading to exclusion from meetings and lack of advancement

- Bad decision making and increased risk taking, leading to business and personal failure

- Physical injuries that require visits to the emergency room

- Misuse of alcohol and drugs

- Arrest and incarceration

- Poor concentration and lessened productivity, leading to problems in school and at work

- Dangerous driving habits

- Aggressive behavior in reaction to normal difficulties

- High blood pressure, heart disease, and stroke

What outcomes have been connected with your anger? Using practice exercise 2, think of one of your anger episodes, and identify the immediate, short-term effects. Try to think of positive outcomes as well as negative ones. And what about long-term outcomes? How do you think this anger episode is likely to affect your relationship(s) with the person(s) involved? What effects might you experience over the longer term?

Harvey's Outcomes: *Demoralized Employees and Digestive Issues*

Over the years, Harvey experienced a number of short- and long-term outcomes of his anger episodes. He found that after he yelled, his employees would show heightened short-term awareness of proper procedures on the sales floor. For a while, fewer mistakes would be made. But human beings are mistake-making creatures; eventually mistakes would once again be made, and Harvey would explode. Over the long term, quite a few of his good employees quit. After all, who would enjoy working in an environment where a demeaning outburst from the boss was a constant possibility? In addition, Harvey's anger eventually brought on major digestive problems (see fig. 2.6).

Part 6. Outcomes

What was a positive short-term outcome of this anger episode?

I noticed that the salespeople seemed to be more on their toes for a while. They made fewer errors.

What was a positive long-term outcome of this anger episode?

None that I can think of.

What was a negative short-term outcome of this anger episode?

I noticed that the salespeople seemed to avoid me after I had one of my angry blowups.

What was a negative long-term outcome of this anger episode?

Two weeks later, my salesperson found another job and quit. She said I was an offensive leader. She was very good, and now I have to replace her. I also have to see my physician about all the stomach problems I've been having.

Figure 2.6. Harvey's Responses to Part 6 of Practice Exercise 2

A Small Assignment

Figure 2.7, at the end of this chapter, shows Harvey's completed Anger Episode Record. After you've reviewed it and used practice exercise 2 to analyze one or more of your own anger episodes, you will have taken the first step toward gaining better control over your anger. To increase your awareness of your anger patterns and gain insight into some important issues, ask yourself the following questions:

- Do my anger episodes usually start with the same type of trigger?

- When I'm angry, what am I usually thinking?

- When I'm angry, what do I usually want to do? What do I usually do?

- How does my anger get rewarded?

- What negative outcomes are associated with my anger episodes?

- What effect is my anger having on my relationships over the long run?

Key Points

☑ Anger episodes follow a predictable six-step pattern: trigger, thoughts, experience, action urge, expression, and outcomes.

☑ The most common trigger for anger is the undesirable behavior of people you know well and like or love.

☑ Anger typically emerges when you distort the trigger or exaggerate its meaning.

☑ Your demandingness is a reflection of your belief that other people must act the way you want them to act. This belief is commonly in force when anger emerges, so be on the alert for it.

☑ Personal experiences of anger vary in terms of anger's frequency, intensity, and duration. How often do you become angry? How strong is your anger? How long does it last?

☑ An action urge (an immediate impulse to act) is influenced by an assortment of factors, such as the context of the trigger, your thoughts, your physical sensations, and your learning history.

☑ Anger can be expressed in many ways. People most frequently express anger verbally, by yelling, arguing, cursing, or making nasty remarks.

☑ The long-term outcomes of anger seem to be the most serious. It is important to consider anger's potential to inflict long-term damage to your relationships, your health, and your happiness.

☑ Increasing your awareness and understanding of your anger episodes is an important first step toward controlling your anger.

Part 1. Trigger

Place a check mark next to the word indicating the area of your life in which your anger was triggered.

___✓___ Work

_____ School

_____ Family

_____ Parenting

___—___ Romantic relationship

_____ Friendship

_____ Other: _____

In one simple sentence, report the event that led to your anger. (Example: "My son forgot again to clean his room.")

For the third time, Maria promised that we would deliver
unavailable roofing shingles in three days.

Part 2. Thoughts

Place a check mark next to any and all statements that apply to this anger episode.

___✓___ Awfulizing: At the time, I thought this was one of the worst things that could be happening.

___✓___ Low frustration tolerance: I thought I could not handle or deal with the situation.

___✓___ Demandingness: I thought the other person(s) should have acted differently.

_____ Rating others: I saw the other person(s) as

_____.

_____ Rating myself: Deep down, I thought I was less important or worthwhile.

_____ Distortion or misinterpretation: My thinking became distorted, and I didn't see things clearly.

Figure 2.7. Harvey's Completed Anger Episode Record

Part 3. Experience

Place a check mark next to the number that corresponds to the intensity of your anger, the extent of your anger, and how you felt in this situation.

Intensity of Your Anger	Extent of Your Anger	How You Felt
_____ 1	Almost no anger	Calm, indifferent
_____ 2	Slight anger	Jarred, moved, stirred, ruffled, challenged
_____ 3 _____ 4	Mild anger	Annoyed, bothered, irritated, perturbed, flustered, uneasy, provoked, impelled, cranky, crotchety, distressed, disturbed
_____ 5 _____ 6	Moderate anger	Mad, agitated, pissed off, irked, aggravated, fired up, riled up, all worked up, peeved, indignant
_____ 7 ✓ 8	Strong anger	Irate, inflamed, exasperated, fuming, burned up, incensed, infuriated, enraged, hysterical
_____ 9 _____ 10	Extreme anger	Frenzied, vicious, unhinged, up in arms, rabid, crazed, maniacal, wild, violent, demented

Now complete the following sentence.

At the time of this specific event, I felt *incensed and furious.*

How long did your anger last?

✓ Minutes   _____ Days

_____ Hours   _____ Ongoing

What physical sensations did you notice?

_____ Fluttering/upset stomach   _____ Sweating

✓ Indigestion   _____ Warmth/flushing

_____ Rapid heart rate   _____ Nausea

_____ Dizziness   _____ Rapid breathing

✓ Fuzziness/feelings of unreality   ✓ Headache

_____ Tingling

_____ Muscle tension   _____ Trembling

_____ Fatigue   _____ Other: _____

Figure 2.7. continued

Part 4. Action Urge

Place a check mark next to the word(s) or phrase(s) corresponding to your action urge(s) in this situation, and briefly describe the impulse that arose for you. (Examples: "I just wanted to get in his face" or "I couldn't wait to got away from her.")

___✓___ Confront

I wanted to confront and verbally blast her.

_____ Withdraw

_____

_____ Resolve the problem

_____

_____ Other

_____

Part 5. Anger Expression

Place a check mark next to any and all behavior you engaged in during this anger episode.

_____ No expression (kept things in, boiled inside, held grudges and didn't tell anyone)

_____ Indirect expression (secretly did something to harm the other person, spread rumors, ignored what the other person wanted)

___✓___ Outward verbal expression (yelled, screamed, argued, threatened; made sarcastic, nasty, or abusive remarks)

_____ Outward expression against an object (broke, threw, slammed, or destroyed an object)

_____ Outward expression against a person (fought, hit, kicked, or shoved someone)

_____ Outward expression through bodily gestures (rolled eyes, crossed arms, glared, frowned, gave a stern look)

___✓___ Avoidance (escaped or walked away from the situation; distracted myself by reading, watching TV, listening to music)

_____ Substance use (drank alcohol; took medications; used other drugs, such as marijuana or cocaine)

_____ Attempt at resolution (compromised, discussed, or came to some agreement with the other person)

_____ Other_____

Figure 2.7. continued

Part 6. Outcomes

What was a positive short-term outcome of this anger episode?

I noticed that the salespeople seemed to be more on their toes for a while. They made fewer errors.

What was a positive long-term outcome of this anger episode?

None that I can think of.

What was a negative short-term outcome of this anger episode?

I noticed that the salespeople seemed to avoid me after I had one of my angry blowups.

What was a negative long-term outcome of this anger episode?

Two weeks later, my salesperson found another job and quit. She said I was an offensive leader. She was very good, and now I have to replace her. I also have to see my physician about all the stomach problems I've been having.

Figure 2.7. continued

CHAPTER 3

Are You Ready to Change?

I wanted to change the world. But I have found that the only thing one can be sure of changing is oneself.

—Aldous Huxley

* A lot of folks say, "I want to stop yelling and screaming. I know it's bad for me and my family" or "I always feel so tense and frustrated. I'd like to let things go more easily." But we've learned that even when people are thinking about changing the way they act when they're angry, that doesn't mean they're ready to do the work that leads to better anger control. Working toward changing how you react to the unwanted events of life requires more than good intentions. It also requires energy and effort. Just reading this book without practicing the new skills you'll learn isn't enough.

It's Your Choice

In this chapter, we invite you to think about your life and consider how you'd answer some personal questions about your motivation to reduce your anger experiences. By the end of the chapter, you'll be able to clearly state your reasons either for wanting to reduce your anger or for staying as you are. You'll also understand your level of readiness and your motivation to work on your anger. If you already know that your anger is a problem, and if you're

* Before you begin this chapter, we recommend that you download practice exercises 3.A (Recognizing Ambivalence About Angry Feelings and Reactions), 3.B (Importance of Reducing Angry Feelings and Reactions), and 3.C (Readiness to Reduce Angry Feelings and Reactions) from http://www.newharbinger.com/42266.

ready to work on anger reduction, you can skip to the next chapter. Nevertheless, we think you're likely to find the ideas in this chapter useful.

Obviously, everybody's life is different. Your own experiences are unique, and since we're not seeing you in person, we can't fully understand your anger. But *you* can! We're simply asking you to look at yourself honestly and decide whether the time has come for you to live your life with less anger.

The reality is that from time to time we all experience unfairness and bad treatment from others. That's just the way the world is. How you choose to react to mistreatment will determine how angry you get, and that in turn will influence the quality of your life. When things go badly, you can certainly continue to get angry. It's your choice. But, as we'll see later, reacting with anger isn't the only option when the difficulties of life emerge.

You can decide if your anger is too frequent, if it's too strong, if it lasts too long, and if it's helpful to you. Other people may be pressuring you to reduce your anger, but no one can really force you to make a change. We think that you have the capacity to examine your circumstances and decide what to do. Throughout this chapter we'll use the example of Sarah to illustrate how to examine your ambivalence toward change, how to evaluate the importance of reducing your anger, and how to determine your readiness to reduce your anger.

Sarah's Self-Awareness and Commitment to Change

Sarah—thirty-eight, divorced, and remarried to a man who had a seven-year-old daughter—continued to share custody of her own eight-year-old son with her ex-husband. Constant quarreling had marked Sarah's first marriage, and Sarah believed that it was her ex who had been responsible for their arguments most of the time.

Sarah's second marriage went well for the first few months. Over time, however, she found herself frequently arguing with her new husband, too. Their conflicts became quite heated. Just as she had done with her first husband, Sarah blamed her second husband for their discord, and she began to doubt whether this new marriage would last. And as the screaming and yelling increased, her son became depressed and withdrawn, and her stepdaughter had tantrums both at home and in school.

After thinking about both her marriages and talking with a close friend, Sarah came to the painful realization that she bore some of the responsibility for the arguing. She also recognized that she didn't want to go through another divorce, nor did she want her young son to experience any more loss.

Sarah was determined to learn how to create a calm and stable home life for herself and her family. She sought counseling, was highly motivated throughout the course of her anger management sessions, and was successful in reducing her angry reactions when things went wrong in the marriage. She still had occasional arguments with her husband, but they were no longer as destructive. She learned not to react so quickly when things were not to her liking, and to adapt to difficult and challenging situations more constructively. These changes on her part led to greater peace in the household, and the behavior of both children improved.

Reasons to Change and Reasons to Stay the Same

What's happening in your life right now that's leading you to think about making a change? Perhaps you're motivated to reduce your angry reactions because you see that others suffer when you yell, scream, withdraw, or pout. Maybe your reactions have led to problems at work, in your family, with your friendships, with your health, or even with the law. These problems may be telling you that change is necessary. It may even be the case that a counselor asked you to read this book as part of an educational program or an intervention. All these reasons for change represent *external* motivations.

In contrast, your motivation to change may be *internal*. You may want to change simply because you would like a more comfortable life and know you can achieve it. You may want to reduce your anger so you can create a calmer and more peaceful home life, enrich your relationships with family members and friends, or improve your chances for advancement at work.

Whatever your motivation for changing your anger experiences, it has two parts:

1.   The recognition that your current anger reactions aren't working

2.   The ability to see a better way of reacting to life's difficulties

Some people *choose* not to change. People who take this approach don't see the downside to their anger. They think of their anger as perfectly appropriate. In fact, seeing their anger as perfectly appropriate is so important to them that they fail to ask themselves if their anger is helping them solve their problems. And, after all, it's easier to create excuses for staying angry than to do the work of making a change.

Other people are concerned about their anger but don't think they *can* change. And to avoid making the effort, they stoically (and stubbornly) accept their current state and deny that anything else is possible.

- "Yeah, my anger sometimes gets me in trouble, but it's no big deal—my wife knows what I'm like."

- "I can't help being angry, and my friends get that."

- "My employees understand why I'm always flying off the handle—it's who I am."

Still others believe that it's *healthy* to express anger. It's true that venting anger can sometimes feel like the right thing to do. It may also provide temporary, illusory relief from an anger-provoking situation. And, unfortunately, our culture has long promoted the idea that cathartic expression is desirable. But experts have largely debunked the notion that if anger is not expressed, it will build up and lead to greater aggression or even to physical illness. Venting anger actually makes people worse, not better.[6]

Additional obstacles to working on anger include beliefs like "My anger gets me what I want" or "My anger protects me." And you certainly can use anger to coerce others into producing the outcomes you desire. But this tactic will usually backfire in the long run because your anger will create resentment and distance in your most valued relationships. Similarly, you can use anger to project a tough image so others will not take advantage of you. But this tactic, too, can have serious drawbacks—you will probably be perceived as a bully, or as someone who is not caring and cannot be trusted with personal information, and these perceptions will lead to less honesty and openness in your personal relationships.

The Big Mistake

- She's always pissing me off.

- My parents make me so angry!

- He constantly provokes me.

- My boss causes me to feel so aggravated!

- My wife makes me blow up at her.

The problem with these types of thoughts is that your focus is on the other person. He or she is the wrongdoer and the cause of your anger, whereas you are the righteous one. But such thoughts won't help you examine the real causes and consequences of your anger and will not lead to change. In fact, we have a phrase for the idea that other people are the sole cause of our anger. We call this idea *the big mistake*.

Angry people who blame others for their emotions are not very concerned about their own actions. Instead, they spend a lifetime playing the blame game. After all, if other people are at fault and are the cause of your anger, then why should *you* have to change? Focusing on the misdeeds of others, no matter how bad those misdeeds may be, allows you to think that holding on to anger is just fine. But, regrettably, no matter how moral, proper, warranted, excusable, or justified your anger may seem to you, it will rarely lead to beneficial changes in others, and you will remain in a state of distress. The big mistake—focusing exclusively on the bad behavior of others—does away with any desire on your part to learn to react differently so that you can become strong, respected, and effective in the world, without excessive anger.

Your Ambivalence Toward Changing

You may not have fully committed yourself to changing your anger. On the one hand, you may recognize the personal pain and costs that accompany your anger. On the other hand, you may have seemingly good reasons and excuses for remaining angry.

It's not at all unusual to feel both ways about your angry reactions. And that's what ambivalence is—the state of feeling two ways about something. This type of wavering is both normal and to be expected when you first consider changing long-standing behavior, emotions, or situations. As psychologists, we've seen ambivalence and indecisiveness in people who are struggling with all sorts of difficulties, including anger. The trick is to understand your own reasons on both sides of the question "Should I deal with my anger?" and make a decision about what's in your best interests over the long run.

Now, using part 1 of practice exercise 3.A, take a closer look at this issue. Once you understand your ambivalence toward reducing your anger, you'll get a better picture of where you stand. We certainly recognize that anger has some benefits, and that there are reasons *not* to change, and to continue being angry. Here, for example, are some remarks from people we've worked with:

- "It feels good to vent my anger. I feel better when I let it out!"

- "If I don't get angry, others will walk all over me."

- "Anger helps me get what I want."

- "When other people treat me badly, my anger helps me express myself."

- "Anger is one way to send a message that other people shouldn't mess with me."

- "What else am I supposed to feel when other people disrespect me? My anger is appropriate!"

- "Anger gives me a feeling of power, and I like that."

- "When I get angry, I'm just giving people what they deserve!"

Sarah's Reasons for Holding On to Anger

When Sarah completed part 1 of practice exercise 3.A, she didn't worry about how many ideas she could come up with. Instead, her goal was simply to identify her major reasons for keeping her anger as it was. She identified three major reasons (see fig. 3.1).

Part 1. Reasons for Holding On to Anger

List your reasons for wanting to hold on to your anger. For example, are there positive aspects to your anger? If so what are they? What other reasons do you have?

My first husband didn't treat me well, and I'm not going to let that happen again.

Sometimes my husband is not considerate. My anger helps me tell him what I want.

If I don't get angry, then my husband won't do things around the house, like cleaning up after the kids.

Figure 3.1. Sarah's Responses to Part 1 of Practice Exercise 3.A

Now, using part 2 of practice exercise 3.A, look at the other side—your reasons for making a change in your reactions and reducing your anger. As we've noted, there are quite a few reasons to work on anger reduction. For you, these may include some of those listed here:

- Improving relationships with your wife or husband, children, and friends

- Increasing your effectiveness at work

- Having closer ties with extended family members

- Wanting less chaos in your life

- Saving your marriage

- Reducing your thoughts about getting even for the perceived negative actions of others

- Reducing your chances of having problems with the criminal justice system

- Lessening the effects of problems with your physical health

- Reducing other negative emotions, such as anxiety and guilt

Think about what your anger is costing you. Don't consider only your most recent or most dramatic anger episodes and problems. Also consider the more subtle and longer-term consequences you've experienced. Obviously, these consequences represent the negative side of the way you act when you're angry and are potential reasons for making a change.

Sarah's Reasons for Reducing Anger

As Sarah completed part 2 of practice exercise 3.A, she kept in mind once again that the point was not to list as many reasons as she could but rather to gain clarity. Sarah identified five reasons for reducing her anger (see fig. 3.2).

> ## Part 2. Reasons for Reducing Anger
>
> Now list your reasons for wanting to reduce your anger. For example, are the costs associated with your anger episodes becoming too high? What other reasons do you have?
>
> The constant bickering is making my marriage negative.
>
> The arguments are upsetting the kids.
>
> I don't feel good when I'm angry.
>
> I want my family life to be calm and peaceful.
>
> I don't want to repeat patterns that did not work well in the past.

Figure 3.2. Sarah's Responses to Part 2 of Practice Exercise 3.A

How Important Changing Is to You

Once you've identified your thoughts on both sides of the issue, it's time to consider how important change is to you. Be thoughtful as you consider this question. Other people may have already complained that your anger drives them away, leads them to feel uncomfortable, or causes disruption at work and in social relationships. It's valuable to consider what others say, but your view is what matters most. Therefore, to guide your thinking, consider how often you become angry, how intense your reactions are, and how long your anger experiences last. Then, using the scale in part 1 of practice exercise 3.B, consider your personal situation, and choose the number between 1 and 7 that best represents how important you think it is to change the way you act when you're angry.

If your rating is 1 or 2, then reducing your anger isn't a high priority for you. It's unlikely that at this time you'll have enough motivation to learn the materials in this book and do the work we suggest. It may be better for you to put this book away for a while and spend some time observing your reactions to the minor annoyances, rejections, disappointments, unfair treatment, and general hassles that are part of life. Examine your reactions to any major problems you experience, too. Pay attention to whether your anger is satisfying, and to whether it brings about the results you want. Examine the short-term outcomes of your anger as well as its likely long-term effects, not just on you but also on others. Does anger work for you? If you're not sure, then keep in mind that motivation to change isn't constant. Rather, it ebbs and flows. Therefore, even if you aren't motivated to work on your anger now, you may well feel different down the road.

If your rating is 3, 4, or 5, then you're moderately committed to reducing your anger. It's likely that there will be periods when you'll focus on the tasks outlined in this book. At other times, however, you may put the required work on the back burner. Most people who struggle with anger rate themselves in this middle range. If that's what you've done, then we suggest that you continue reading. It's likely that you'll be able to make effective use of this book.

The Importance to Sarah of Reducing Her Anger

Like most other people who are wondering whether they should work on their anger, Sarah indicated in part 1 of practice exercise 3.B that changing her angry behavior was moderately important to her (see fig. 3.3).

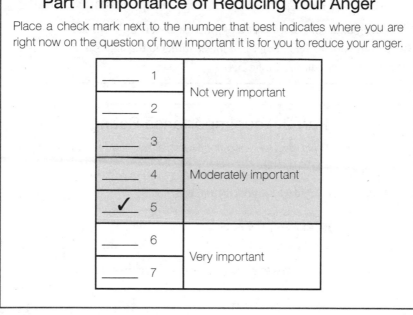

Figure 3.3. Sarah's Response to Part 1 of Practice Exercise 3.B

And now we come to something of a trick question. Using part 2 of practice exercise 3.B, consider why you didn't give a *lower* rating to the importance of changing. Your answer will reveal why reducing your anger actually *is* important to you. After all, anyone who thinks that anger reduction isn't very important will give a rating of 1 or 2 to the issue of importance. Therefore, if your rating was higher than 1 or 2, you may be more motivated to change than you realized.

If your importance rating is 6 or 7, you obviously think that a change in your behavior is essential. You're probably ready to commit yourself to learning and completing this book. Keep in mind, however, that even though your commitment to change is high, your motivation can fluctuate. To reinforce your own reasons for change, answer the following question: "Why did I rate the importance of change so highly?" Again, your answer is likely to show you a clear reason for your rating. As you read through (or reread) each chapter of this book, remind yourself why completing the book and working with its exercises is aligned with what you think is important in life and with your goals for self-improvement.

Sarah's Thoughts About Her Importance Rating

When Sarah considered part 2 of practice exercise 3.B, she listed two reasons why she had not given a lower rating to the importance of controlling her anger (see fig. 3.4).

Part 2. Your Importance Rating

Why didn't you give a lower rating (for example, a rating of 1) to the importance of reducing your anger?

A peaceful home life is a priority for me.

The arguing is harming the kids.

Figure 3.4. Sarah's Responses to Part 2 of Practice Exercise 3.B

How Ready You Are to Change

Why now? You may recognize that it's important to reduce your anger, but you may or may not think that this is the time to do it. Some people have told us that they're not ready to work on their anger because they don't believe they have the time or the energy to give it their best effort. We agree that timing is important. It may be unwise to consider using this book if you have too many pressing commitments and obligations. At the same time, conditions are rarely perfect.

You may be telling yourself you can work on anger reduction at a later time. On the surface, it often appears easier not to face problems, and to put things off. In actuality, not facing problems is much more difficult in the long run. It usually takes much less energy and effort to reduce your anger than it does to manage your life with your problem-causing angry ways, not to mention the resulting chaos. We recognize that wanting to put things off is normal. And we all procrastinate. But the good news is that, over time, the arguments for dealing with a problem often become stronger than the arguments for avoiding it, and people eventually take the necessary steps to make their lives better. The key is to change *before* the difficulties associated with your behavior create severe problems in your life.

How ready are you to work on your anger? Using the scale in part 1 of practice exercise 3.C, consider your personal situation, and choose the number between 1 and 7 that best represents how ready you are to change the way you act when you're angry.

If your readiness rating is 1 or 2, then you don't yet have a strong desire to bring your anger under control. Try to figure out if that's because you just have too many current commitments or if it's because you want to avoid facing your problems involving anger. If you believe that you're truly too busy right now, designate a time in the future when you'll be able to give the ideas in this book a reasonable effort. But if you think your lack of readiness has more to do with avoidance, ask yourself the following question: "What types of bad things would have to happen to make me want to change my anger reactions?"

Discomfort, along with the recognition that there's a problem, can often instigate change. It's possible that your anger hasn't yet led to much loss or pain. Therefore, your anger may not seem to be much of a problem. Perhaps your marriage still seems intact, and although you haven't been promoted at work, at least you haven't been fired. Perhaps your friends are still with you, but they may have become more like distant acquaintances. And perhaps you're blaming the problems you're having with your children on their school or on their friends rather than recognizing your part in what's happening. Your answer reveals the types of losses or costs that are meaningful to you and that could influence your decision to work on anger control. Only you can decide if the right time is now.

A readiness rating of 3, 4, or 5 indicates that there are times when you clearly see your anger as a concern. At other times, it doesn't seem to bother you so much. Again, most people fall into this middle range and can expect their readiness to waver somewhat.

Sarah's Readiness to Change

In part 1 of practice exercise 3.C, Sarah gave her readiness a rating of 4 (see fig. 3.5). With this rating, she indicated her moderate readiness to change.

Part 1. Your Readiness to Reduce Anger

Place a check mark next to the number that best indicates where you are right now on the question of your readiness to take steps toward reducing your anger.

_____ 1	Not very important
_____ 2	
_____ 3	Moderately important
___✓___ 4	
_____ 5	
_____ 6	Very important
_____ 7	

Figure 3.5. Sarah's Response to Part 1 of Exercise 3.C

And here's that trick question again. Using part 2 of practice exercise 3.C, consider why you didn't give a *lower* rating to your readiness for change. Your answer will highlight why change actually is important to you right now. After all, if you didn't find working on your anger somewhat pressing, you would have given a lower rating to your readiness. As you examine your life and look ahead, it's worthwhile to be aware of why reducing your anger may be urgent. Recognition of the costs of your anger will increase your readiness to work on it.

If your readiness rating is 6 or 7, now is clearly the time to commit yourself to getting the help offered by this book. It's important to strike while the iron is hot. But, again, make sure your reasoning is crystal clear by answering this question: "Why did I rate my readiness to reduce my anger so highly?" Your answer will clarify the concerns that have brought you to the point of being ready to take steps toward change.

Sarah's Thoughts About Her Readiness Rating

When Sarah considered part 2 of practice exercise 3.C, she offered two reasons for not giving a lower rating to her readiness to control her anger (see fig. 3.6).

Part 2. Your Readiness Rating

Why didn't you give a lower rating (for example, a rating of 1) to your readiness to take steps toward reducing your anger?

I want to improve things before they get worse.

If I wait too long, it might be too late.

Figure 3.6. Sarah's Responses to Part 2 of Exercise 3.C

Is Anger Working for You?

There are a lot of good reasons for reducing frequent, intense, long-term anger reactions, and there are a few for staying as you are. What we're asking you to do is examine your life to see if becoming angry works for you. To do that, you don't need to have given a rating of 6 or 7 to the importance of changing or to your readiness for change. Completing the practice exercises for this chapter can be helpful in making your reasons for change obvious to you (figure 3.7, at the end of this chapter, gathers Sarah's responses to this chapter's practice exercises). We hope that thinking about the questions we've posed in this chapter has given you clearer insight into your own arguments for change.

As we mentioned earlier, however, motivation fluctuates. You may be less motivated to change during a period of relative calm, but your motivation may quickly increase after a blowup that brings negative consequences (disruption in your family, loss of a friend or a job, a run-in with the law). The best way to deal with variations in motivation is to consider the *long-term benefits* of changing as opposed to staying as you are.

Key Points

☑ Even if others are pressuring you to be less angry, deciding to change is *your* choice.

☑ The big mistake is to focus exclusively on the bad behavior of others while ignoring the more important question of whether your anger is working to make your life better.

☑ Being ambivalent means feeling two opposite ways at the same time. It's normal to be ambivalent about changing your anger.

☑ When your anger is excessive and disruptive, it takes far more energy to manage your life than to make a change.

☑ It's helpful to consider what is at stake if you *don't* reduce your anger.

☑ It's helpful to consider the three best reasons you have for reducing your angry feelings and reactions.

Part 1. Reasons for Holding On to Anger

List your reasons for wanting to hold on to your anger. For example, are there positive aspects to your anger? If so what are they? What other reasons do you have?

My first husband didn't treat me well, and I'm not going to let that happen again.

Sometimes my husband is not considerate. My anger helps me tell him what I want.

If I don't get angry, then my husband won't do things around the house, like cleaning up after the kids.

Part 2. Reasons for Reducing Anger

Now list your reasons for wanting to reduce your anger. For example, are the costs associated with your anger episodes becoming too high? What other reasons do you have?

The constant bickering is making my marriage negative.

The arguments are upsetting the kids.

I don't feel good when I'm angry.

I want my family life to be calm and peaceful.

I don't want to repeat patterns that did not work well in the past.

Figure 3.7. Sarah's Complete Responses to Practice Exercises 3.A, 3.B, and 3.C

Part 1. Importance of Reducing Your Anger

Place a check mark next to the number that best indicates where you are right now on the question of how important it is for you to reduce your anger.

_____ 1	Not very important
_____ 2	
_____ 3	Moderately important
_____ 4	
✓ _____ 5	
_____ 6	Very important
_____ 7	

Part 2. Your Importance Rating

Why didn't you give a lower rating (for example, a rating of 1) to the importance of reducing your anger?

A peaceful home life is a priority for me.

The arguing is harming the kids.

Figure 3.7. continued

Part 1. Your Readiness to Reduce Anger

Place a check mark next to the number that best indicates where you are right now on the question of your readiness to take steps toward reducing your anger.

_____ 1	Not very important
_____ 2	
_____ 3	Moderately important
✓ 4	
_____ 5	
_____ 6	Very important
_____ 7	

Part 2. Your Readiness Rating

Why didn't you give a lower rating (for example, a rating of 1) to your readiness to take steps toward reducing your anger?

I want to improve things before they get worse.

If I wait too long, it might be too late.

Figure 3.7. continued

PART 2

Changing Anger Triggers

CHAPTER 4

Strategy One:
Manage Your Lifestyle

It is a common experience that a problem difficult at night is resolved in the morning, after the committee of sleep has worked on it.

—John Steinbeck

When we look for the causes of our anger, most of us probably don't give much consideration to lifestyle and environmental factors. In this chapter, we ask you to look at managing your habits and your environment as a first step toward reducing your anger reactions. We also provide some suggestions to help you address those issues.

Habits and Environmental Factors

Don't laugh, but have you ever considered the effect of the weather on your personality and interactions with other people? Researchers from Columbia University have reported that people living in climates with an average temperature of about 72 degrees Fahrenheit had high scores on agreeability, emotional stability, extroversion, and openness to experience—all very useful characteristics for anyone dealing with conflict or feeling disrespected, rejected, or neglected—and that as temperatures become hotter, or cooler, these positive personality factors typically decreased.[7] There certainly are personal variations in our responses to heat, but anger and conflict do tend to rise with the temperature, and crime rates go up in the hotter months. Indeed, on a sweltering summer day, aren't you more likely to honk at someone who cuts you off in traffic than you are on a temperate spring day?

Likewise, you can see your own anger episodes as wildfires. Are there factors that make it more likely for one of your anger wildfires to ignite? This is the type of question addressed by the fields of environmental psychology and biological psychology, both of which offer important insights into how you can rearrange your daily world in ways that make angry, aversive interactions less likely. Sometimes, for example, it can be helpful to simply delay a potentially problematic interaction until the heat of the day has passed, or until after lunch or dinner. And sometimes reducing alcohol use or investing in an air conditioner can bring peace to a quarreling family. In the sections that follow, we discuss the lifestyle and environmental factors that most commonly serve as kindling for anger wildfires.

Food and Nutrition

Ah, the sweetness of sugary desserts! How wonderful at the end of a meal! Unfortunately, however, certain types of food (such as sweets) may contribute to the development of anger. Many psychologists and nutritionists blame too many simple carbohydrates as well as deficiencies in magnesium (which helps the muscles relax) and deficiencies in various other minerals and vitamins. They suggest that people who live mostly on processed foods, white flour, and white sugar are more likely to experience anger than people who consume large amounts of fruits, leafy greens, and beans. These ideas may seem a little odd to you, but there is good scientific evidence that the kinds of foods you eat can increase or decrease your likelihood of becoming angry when things don't go your way.

Have you ever heard the word "hanger"? It's a combination of the words "hunger" and "anger," and it refers to the kind of irritability you may experience when you are hungry. Let us explain this a bit. The foods you eat are broken down by your digestive system into simple sugars (mostly what is known as *glucose*) and fatty acids. Glucose then enters your bloodstream (the amount of glucose circulating in your blood at any given time is called your *blood glucose level*), and eventually the glucose goes to your organs and tissues, where it is used for energy. So far, so good. Eventually, however, your blood glucose level drops. When this happens, you may still be able to act reasonably in an important situation, such as a business meeting or a class at school. But in a casual situation, where your guard is down and you feel less constrained, you may become irritable and lose patience with others as your blood glucose level plummets, and your angry urges may be more likely to surface.

To remedy the situation, you may reach for a candy bar or some other sugary treat, or for a simple carbohydrate like a bag of potato chips, mistakenly thinking that this is the way to reduce your discomfort. But what you really need, especially on an empty stomach, is the type of protein or complex carbohydrate that breaks down into glucose more slowly and provides a steadier, longer-lasting amount of glucose in your bloodstream. Nevertheless, we don't always make or understand these connections. So reaching for candy or a cookie can become a habit, one that partially accounts for some of the weight gain many of us experience as we age and our bodily systems become somewhat less efficient.

But there's another problem with "hanger," and it's at least as serious as weight gain. When your blood glucose level drops too much, your body compensates by releasing adrenaline and cortisol, the same hormones that are released when you feel threatened. These hormones make you overly sensitive to others' negative remarks and actions, and they initiate your body's fight-or-flight response, even though you're not actually facing a real threat. "Hanger" is probably part of an evolutionary mechanism. When our animal ancestors experienced a drop in blood glucose level, they had to get food into their bodies in order to survive. For them, being self-centered, angry, and aggressive meant getting more food and resolving a life-or-death situation. But here's a bottom line for us in the twenty-first century: when it comes to managing conflict and adversity over the course of a day, a steady blood glucose level is better than a quick jolt of energy that quickly dissipates.

As we've suggested, some foods are especially likely to be associated with a quick jolt of energy (that is, an immediate spike in blood glucose level) that rapidly dissipates. These foods are said to have a *high glycemic load*. They may be tasty and seem filling, and you may feel good immediately after eating them, but they will rather quickly put you into a state where your blood glucose level drops so low that you have trouble controlling your emotional reactions. Other foods, said to have a *low glycemic load*, produce a longer and steadier blood glucose level as well as steadier thinking and less "hanger." Table 4.1 is a glycemic load chart.

Table 4.1. Foods with Lower and Higher Glycemic Load (GL)

Lower GL	Higher GL
Apple (6)	Bagel, white, frozen (25)
Bran cereal (4)	Cola (15)
Baked beans (7)	Cornflakes (21)
Barley, coarse (7)	Couscous (23)
Black beans (7)	Cranberry juice (24)
Cashews, salted (3)	Cream of wheat, instant (22)
Grapefruit (3)	Dates (42)
Hamburger bun (9)	Kugel (egg noodles, sugar, cheese) (31)
Hummus (chickpea salad dip) (0)	Macaroni; macaroni and cheese (32)
Ice cream, full fat, average serving (8)	Pizza, cheese and tomato sauce (22)
Microwave popcorn (8)	Potato, baked (26)
Milk, full fat (3)	Rice, quick-cooking white basmati (23)
Milk, skim (4)	Raisins (28)
Peach (5)	Sirloin chop, vegetables, potato (35)
Pear (4)	Spaghetti (26)
Peanuts (1)	Strawberry processed-fruit bar (23)
Pumpernickel bread (6)	Toaster pastry, double chocolate (25)
Tomato juice, canned, no sugar added (4)	Vanilla-flavored cake (24)
Wheat tortilla (8)	
Watermelon (4)	

Note: A GL of 10 or lower is judged to have a very small effect on blood glucose level, whereas a GL of 20 or higher can lead to a very quick spike and correspondingly rapid drop in blood glucose level; a GL of 11 to 19 has a moderate impact on blood glucose level. For more information, see "Glycemic Index for 60+ Foods," Harvard Health Publishing, Harvard Medical School, 2015, retrieved from https://www.health.harvard.edu/diseases-and-conditions/glycemic-index-and-glycemic-load-for-100-foods, updated 14 March 2018.

All this information brings us to two recommendations we would like you to consider:

1. If you become angry more often than you would like, be thoughtful about what you eat. Include more foods in your diet that have a lower glycemic load. They provide a more even level of glucose in your bloodstream and will give you a better chance of responding to disappointments, conflicts, and adversity without anger. Of course, there are other considerations to take into account. You may be on a low-carbohydrate diet, or you may have dietary restrictions connected to your religion. Or you may be diabetic, in which case we suggest that you consult with your physician or a professional dietitian. Also remember that table 4.1 is based on typical portions. One hamburger bun or a few peanuts may be just fine for you; three buns and a whole jar of peanuts are something else.

2. Be thoughtful about *when* you face difficult situations or talk to others about resolving potential conflicts, and about *when* you interact with the difficult people in your life. You may find that you can develop better solutions to marital or family conflicts, or occupational disappointments, if you discuss such problems after a meal, when your blood glucose level is adequate and stable. It turns out that there's wisdom in that old piece of advice to eat a healthy breakfast before going to work or school.

Alcohol

Alcohol affects people differently, and so you would be wise to consider your own reactions to beer, wine, and liquor. Some folks who drink to excess at dinnertime become lethargic and nonreactive to social interaction. They just go to bed early. Others become argumentative and even aggressive.

Louis, a married thirty-four-year-old locksmith with an eight-year-old daughter, had a true anger problem that was connected to alcohol use. In the early years of his marriage, he came home straight from work to be with his wife. He would have a beer at dinner, with no additional drinking after that. Over time, however, his routine had evolved to stopping at a local bar with co-workers before coming home. He would then have a few beers with dinner, and later in the evening he drank whiskey.

Unfortunately, Louis's anger and aggression toward his wife and their daughter increased when he became intoxicated. He became less patient and tolerant of mistakes and was not receptive to questions or feedback of any sort. When inebriated, he had a tendency to interpret many of his wife's comments as criticisms.

In the beginning, his intoxicated anger episodes had resulted mostly in verbal rants and noisy arguments laced with profanities, but eventually he began to break household objects and push his wife and their daughter. They became frightened, never quite knowing what would set him off.

Louis's wife finally divorced him after several years of walking on eggshells, a period during which Louis was arrested twice. Because their daughter reacted with marked anxiety whenever Louis got near her, his wife obtained a protective order that prohibited him from visiting the household. Louis was allowed only supervised visits with his daughter, and a social worker had to be present.

After the divorce, Louis moved to a small apartment, where in time he began to live with a new girlfriend. He continued to drink, and he was never promoted at work. He had frequent arguments with his girlfriend about his lack of professional advancement and his lack of motivation to improve his life, and these arguments marred their relationship.

The link between anger and increased substance use is clear. One explanation for this link is that people who experience chronic anger turn to alcohol (and sometimes other drugs) as a means of reducing their negative internal activation and agitation. Over time, according to this explanation, the pattern becomes entrenched (that is, drinking gets reinforced) because alcohol consistently dulls the unpleasant bodily experiences that accompany chronic anger. Another explanation is that alcohol reduces some people's inhibitions and thus increases their verbal and physical expressions of anger. Consciously, these people feel more confident when they're buzzed, and so they're more likely to let their anger out in destructive ways. In addition, alcohol impairs the functioning of that portion of the brain known as the *prefrontal cortex*, responsible for what is called *executive decision making*. The prefrontal cortex comes into play when we perceive a threat or a conflict (as when we think we have been insulted or demeaned), and it enables us to consider all the possible outcomes related to a situation before we make a decision about how to react.

Overall, it seems that alcohol use and anger have a reciprocal relationship. Drinking can lead to more anger, and anger can lead to more drinking. It's a vicious cycle. The good news is that anger management interventions can lead to reductions in problematic drinking. For example, in 2006 our colleague Jerry Deffenbacher had a group of alcoholic men and women receive either a six-month Alcoholics Anonymous–related treatment or an alcohol-adapted anger management treatment; at the end of treatment, the people in both groups showed significant reductions in drinking and anger.[8]

But this is not a book about alcoholism or treatment for excessive drinking, and we don't want to stray too far into that area. We just want to highlight the importance of knowing yourself and living the most successful life you can. If it seems to you that your drinking habits are leading to angry interactions with others, take steps to bring your alcohol use under control. It's true that looking honestly at your drinking habits can be difficult, and it's common for people to minimize the effects that alcohol has on their lives. We frequently hear statements like "My drinking has nothing to do with my family problems. If my wife would just treat me with more respect, I wouldn't blow up at her the way I do." Excessive alcohol intake can also be associated with anxiety, shame, guilt, and other forms of emotional distress. We're just asking you to monitor your alcohol use and consider how it may be reducing your ability to cope with conflict, disappointment, and stress. You may or may not find your alcohol use to be a habit that would be helpful for you to work on. If you do, see the resources for managing your substance use in appendix A.

Sleep

Research with healthy adolescents, male prison inmates, juvenile offenders, and others indicates that poor or inadequate sleep is associated with anger and aggression. Sleep problems also seem to be important in cases of intimate partner violence, bullying at school, cyberbullying, and violence committed in psychiatric hospitals. But most of us already know that lack of sleep can lead to all sorts of problems, and general irritability is one. And just as we have the word "hanger" for the irritability that can accompany hunger, we have the word "slanger" for the irritability that can accompany sleep deprivation.

There are wide variations in the need for sleep. Most people get about six and a half hours per night. Yet most of us desire about eight hours each night, and eight hours seems to be the amount of sleep that helps us function at our best.[9] But if most people are sleeping only about six and a half hours per night, then most are functioning with a nightly sleep deficit of about ninety minutes.

Work is one factor that can influence our sleep habits. In a 2014 Gallup poll, 21 percent of adult respondents in the United States reported working fifty to fifty-nine hours per week, and 25 percent of salaried respondents said they worked more than sixty hours per week; the average number of work hours for all respondents was forty-nine—one full day more than the imagined forty-hour work week—and 13 percent of respondents reported having more than one job.[10] You probably know many people who work so hard that they have little time to devote to personal and family issues, and to sleep.

A related fact is that many adults work evening, night, or rotating shifts; that is, they may work a shift that runs from nine in the morning to six in the evening one day, a shift that runs from midnight to eight in the morning the following day, and so forth.[11] This group includes airline personnel, emergency room doctors, police officers, firefighters, restaurant waitstaff, and combat personnel. And, of course, mothers and fathers and other caregivers also fall into this category. College students regularly do not get adequate sleep because of academic responsibilities or social events, and older adults typically get less sleep than they did in their earlier years. These days of globalization and the twenty-four-hour-per-day economy certainly don't help.

There is a rather strong relationship between lack of sleep and the tendency to respond with anger when things go wrong. Sleep deprivation, in addition to increasing irritability and anger, can contribute to depression, headaches, memory problems, concentration difficulties, ulcers, heart disease, and occupational accidents.

The connection between sleep disturbances and anger seems to be related to disruptions in the normal circadian rhythm patterns. Human beings, other animals, and even plants and bacteria respond predictably to built-in, genetically determined, twenty-four-hour cycles. We are programmed to be most alert in the daylight hours and to sleep in darkness. We are most alert in the morning. We are most coordinated and have the greatest muscle strength from midafternoon to late afternoon, and we are in the stage of deepest sleep at about two in the morning. At about seven in the morning our blood pressure rises, and there is an end to the secretion of melatonin, which helps us sleep. When this rhythm is disrupted, the likelihood of anger and aggression increases. At the behavioral level, when sleep is disrupted we see a worsening of cognitive performance, poorer decision making, and impulsiveness.

So what can you do?

1. Recognize that "slanger" is a real problem.

2. Don't take on important tasks that are highly complex or frustrating when you are short on sleep.

3. Don't interact with difficult people or engage in challenging social interactions when you are short on sleep.

You may not realize that your emotional reactions will be worse after a night of minimal or poor sleep, but they will be. Simple awareness about the effects of sleep is important, since this kind of awareness can help you think more clearly about when it's best for you to interact with others or take on challenging scenarios. We understand that for some people (and maybe you're one of them) it may be difficult to adjust sleep patterns because of work, school, or childrearing responsibilities, but many life adjustments may still be possible (see "Improving Sleep").

Improving Sleep

Eating and Drinking

- Don't eat a big meal right before bedtime because it may prevent deep sleep. Consider making lunch your big meal of the day.

- Alcohol makes most folks sleepy, but after a few hours it wakes you up. So don't drink alcohol before bedtime.

- Drinking anything at all before bedtime is a bad idea, since you'll probably need to urinate a few hours later. So don't drink liquids within three hours of going to sleep.

- Be careful about consuming caffeine too close to bedtime. Coffee, sodas, some kinds of ice cream, energy water, and chocolate are some of the major offenders. Even decaffeinated coffee typically contains some caffeine. Also be careful of pain relievers and cold medicines because they often contain caffeine. Try noncaffeinated tea.

Light and Noise

- Power down your electronics before bedtime. A cell phone, a tablet, a computer, a TV, or a digital clock near your bed typically creates a blue light that interferes with sleep. Turn your electronics off, dim them, or set them, if you can, to a mode that produces a warmer light.

- Do you really need a bedside alarm clock? You may end up checking it repeatedly during the night if you're worried about a business meeting or an academic exam the next day. Show faith in your alarm clock! Place it out of sight—in the next room, under the bed, or in a drawer, where you can hear the alarm without seeing the face of the clock.

- Keep noise to a minimum. If there are distractions in your home, see if a white noise machine will help.

- Do not make or accept phone calls, send or read text messages, or engage in electronic chats during your sleep hours.

Bedroom Hygiene

- If possible, go to sleep and wake up at roughly the same time every day. This regular schedule will help your brain and body get used to being on a healthy sleep-wake schedule.

- Your bed is for sleeping. Do not do work, watch TV, play games, or eat in bed.

- Keep your bed clean, and keep pets off the bed. Mites, molds, dander, and other allergens can activate allergies, which will surely keep you up.

- Adjust your bedroom temperature. For most people, the best temperature range for sleeping is 68 to 72 degrees.

Exercise and Pain

- Vigorous exercise is great—but not right before bedtime. It excites you, just when you want to be calm.

- Minor back pain may not wake you up, but it can disturb deeper sleep. Some people find that a pillow between their legs helps.

- Check pain medications with your physician.

Thoughts for Shift Workers

- Try not to work two or more night shifts in a row. You're more likely to recover if you can schedule days off between your shifts.

- When you can, avoid frequently rotating shifts. If that is impossible, it is usually easier to adjust to a schedule that rotates from a day shift to an evening shift to a night shift rather than going in the reverse order.

- Keep your workplace brightly lighted to promote alertness. It may be helpful to try a bright-light box. Your body has an internal clock that tells you when to be awake and when to be asleep, and that internal clock is controlled by light. Most of us wake up to light and go to sleep when it's dark. Light is associated with alertness.

- Use blackout blinds or heavy curtains to block sunlight when you sleep during the day. One of the strongest stimulators of your internal wake-up alarm is sunlight. It goes right through your eyelids and stimulates you to stay awake.

Music

Music has been used forever to affect mood. The drums of war intensify aggression, and a devotional chant soothes the soul. We listen to music both to relax and to step up a physical workout.

When elevators were new, they were filled with calming music intended to ease the anxiety of passengers. This practice led to the term "elevator music." This type of music originally had a utilitarian purpose—to encourage the use of elevators. As a term, "elevator music" now refers in general to bland, low-volume recorded music played in public places like shopping malls. It's also known as "piped-in music," "easy-listening music," "Muzak," and "background music," and it's not intended to be the listener's main focus. Background music may reduce anxiety, improve attention and memory, and even enhance short-term learning. One possible explanation of these effects is that background music can increase arousal and promote a positive emotional state, which then sharpens attention to details. For these effects to occur, however, the music has to be true background music, with minimal variation in tempo and loudness, and with no distracting lyrics. Other musical genres, such as rap, heavy metal, and emo (emotional hardcore), typically have a faster tempo and are played loudly. There is a great deal of variation among these genres, but they may contain aggressive and sexually explicit lyrics, often including profanity and focusing on serious social issues.

Given the wide range of people's taste in music, there are many reasons to appreciate different musical genres. But it's also likely that different genres produce different effects.

Eugene, a twenty-four-year-old auto parts salesperson, typically listened to loud, aggressive music during his thirty-minute drive to work. By the time he got there, he was ready for action. On the upside, he was energized and ready to greet customers. On the downside, he was often impulsive and disrespectful in his interactions with customers. They found him to be annoying. Eventually Eugene was given fewer work hours. Finally he was fired because of complaints about his attitude.

The effects of a musical genre may be due to loudness or tempo or lyrics. For example, researchers who placed subjects in a driving simulator where they were exposed to frustrating situations while listening to either positive or negative high- or low-energy music found that more anger and higher blood pressure were associated with high-energy negative music.[12] Other research showed that listening to songs with violent lyrics increased hostility as well as aggressive thoughts and feelings.[13] On a more positive note, still other researchers have found that when prisoners listened to relaxing music their anger and anxiety were reduced, and that listening to either sad or happy music was associated with fewer errors in driving.[14]

We are not making a case against more active forms of music. We are simply noting that many of us live in chaotic households with screaming children, argumentative spouses, barking dogs, and computers and television sets that are constantly on. If this kind of household sounds like yours, then we suggest that you turn off the television or the computer and consider playing soft, pleasant music without lyrics when you're at home. It costs very little to take these steps, and the possible payoff, in terms of less conflict and more inner peace, is high. We also favor adding soft, slow, pleasant music to many work or institutional environments where anger reduction is a goal. Finally, consider the type of music you listen to while driving. In many areas, roads are heavily trafficked and filled with inconsiderate drivers. Listening to calming music may be helpful. There's really no good reason not to try it.

Colors and Smells

What about the positive power of colors, smells, and, of course, flowers? One study found that men and women who gave flowers were perceived as happy, achieving, capable, and emotionally intelligent, and that they presented the impression of being able to express their feelings effectively while taking time to understand the feelings of others; as part of the same study, women who received flowers reported a positive mood that sometimes lasted for days.[15] Perceptions and reactions like these show how flowers can easily play a role in improving a relationship.

Charlotte and Carl, thirty-five and thirty-six, respectively, had a marriage that was relatively stable except for their daily bickering. They both worked full-time at high-stress jobs in the financial industry. Charlotte was a stock analyst, and Carl was a banker.

By the time they came home at night, they were totally fatigued. Often, for little or no reason, they would snap at each other and trade mild verbal putdowns. They both complained about the messiness of their apartment, about the trash that had to be taken out, and about such other obligations as paying bills, hiring an electrician to fix broken switches, and so on. And each of them often blamed the other for not taking care of these problems.

One day Charlotte stopped on her way home from work and bought a medium-size bouquet with a strong fragrance. She thought she had done this for herself, but she was surprised when Carl noticed the flowers and said how beautiful they were.

Soon enough, Charlotte and Carl regularly had flowers on their dinner table, and this change seemed to elevate their conversations and reduce their bickering. Many factors probably contributed to the improvement in their relationship—for example, they also repainted their living room a soothing shade of medium blue—but the beneficial effects of the flowers cannot be overlooked.

People vary in their reactions to specific colors, but certain effects seem to be universal, and some scientists think that's because colors directly stimulate structures in the brain:

- Colors at the red end of the spectrum are considered warm and include orange and yellow in addition to red. In many people, these colors elicit reactions that range from a sense of warmth and comfort to the opposite—anger and hostility.

- Colors in the blue area of the spectrum are considered cool and include purple and green in addition to blue. People often react to these colors with calmness or sadness.

- Black has traditionally been associated with formality, unhappiness, and death.

Of course, some people don't react to color, and a few may be color blind, but the idea that particular colors produce certain effects is supported by research and is not to be ignored:

- In one study, the walls of a classroom were repainted from orange and white to royal blue and light blue, the classroom's orange rug was replaced with a gray carpet, and fluorescent lights were exchanged for full-spectrum lighting.[16] After these changes were made, the average systolic blood pressure of the children in the classroom dropped from 120 to 100, they were better behaved, and they showed a decrease in sadness and aggression on mood measures.

- In a study called the Blue Room Experiment, some inmates in solitary confinement at Oregon's Snake River Correctional Institute were given an opportunity to watch nature videos projected onto a wall for about one hour per day.[17] These inmates ended up committing 26 percent fewer acts of violence and self-injury, and fewer forced cell extractions were required. When other inmates began to show signs of emerging anger and violence, such as pacing and rocking, they were taken to the Blue Room to de-escalate their negative behavior.

- Researchers in the United Kingdom placed adult subjects in a driving simulator with simulated traffic jams and exposed some of the subjects to blue light.[18] The subjects exposed to blue light reported less anger than the other subjects. In addition, subjects exposed to blue light had lower systolic blood pressure and reduced muscular activity. The researchers concluded that anger generated by an uncontrollable situation, such as a traffic jam, can be detrimental to health and that exposure to blue light can reduce unhealthful effects.

Lighting

There was a time in the 1970s when architects designed buildings without windows, aiming to achieve better temperature control and reduce external noise, and hoping to enhance learning in educational facilities. In retrospect, that approach was not wise. Most of us prefer natural light that streams through windows, and we respond better to full-spectrum electrical lighting than to fluorescent lighting or other limited sources of light. Full-spectrum lighting may help improve mood and increase motivation. These effects in turn can increase resilience in the face of disappointment, rejection, and other kinds of adversity. If you are in the process of designing a home, an office, or a work or family structure of any sort, we recommend natural lighting.

Key Points

☑ As you take the journey toward reducing your anger, think about what you may be able to change in your everyday routines and environment.

☑ Plan activities and interactions for times when you have eaten properly and slept well.

☑ Alcohol can reduce your tolerance for distress, so be honest about your drinking patterns and determine whether they are fueling your anger and affecting your relationships with colleagues, friends, or family members.

☑ A pleasant environment filled with calming music, nice smells, soothing colors, and natural or full-spectrum lighting will make the world seem more appealing and allow you to deal more effectively with conflict, rejection, disappointment, and other sources of discomfort.

☑ You can take positive steps that will improve your lifestyle.

CHAPTER 5

Strategy Two:
Sidestep Provocations

You can't wrestle with a chimney sweep and come out clean.

—Charles Adams

* It may seem weak or cowardly to avoid a problem. And, indeed, it's good to face some problems head-on and not hide from life's difficulties. For example, we know it's important to talk to our children about bad grades, inappropriate friends, sex, drugs, and the like, just as we know we'll eventually have to talk to the husband or wife we suspect of having an affair, to business partners who aren't carrying their load, to the friend who gossips, or to the neighbor who has loud parties that continue late into the night. In these cases, we're dealing with a relationship that is likely to continue for a long time, and where an eventual resolution is important. But if you consider your anger reactions thoughtfully, you will realize that in many situations there's little benefit to immediately confronting the person or event that has triggered your anger. It's true that continued anger can poison your relationships and your health, but in the long run it may be better to avoid some people or situations until you've developed the skills to deal with them. This may seem like the easy way out, but if you want to live a happy life, it's unwise to immediately confront problems without forethought and planning. We suggest that you sidestep some anger-producing situations by using avoidance or escape as a simple and concrete first step toward breaking up angry

* Before you begin this chapter, we recommend that you download practice exercise 5 (Avoiding and Escaping from Anger Triggers) from http://www.newharbinger.com/42266.

reaction patterns. Avoidance and escape are two different practices: to *avoid* something means to anticipate a problem and intentionally refrain from contact with a person or a situation if you're likely to become angry; to *escape* means to remove yourself from a situation after a problem has appeared and you've noticed that your anger is building.

Choosing Your Battles

This chapter revolves around three key questions:

1. *Which* problematic people and situations are worth dealing with?

2. *When* should a problematic person or situation be confronted?

3. *How* should a problematic person or situation be confronted?

Knowing the answers to these three questions is your best bet for finding temporary relief from anger and moving toward a calmer and happier life.

Which Problems?

Does every problem really need to be addressed? Do you really have to tell off a rude taxi driver? Do you have to confront a slow and unhelpful salesperson? Must you give a piece of your mind to a person who cuts in line? Is it your job to make drivers who cut you off see the error of their ways? You may experience some annoyance in these situations, but you'd be wise to decide whether taking an angry action will actually accomplish anything. If a resolution is possible and can lead to better behavior in the future, then it may be worth your time and energy to resolve an issue. But if you'll never see the other person again, or never again face the same problem, you may be better off just walking away.

When to Confront?

Is the moment when you're feeling angriest the best time to address a particular problem? Too many people give in to the urge to act impulsively. When an adverse and potentially angering event occurs, you can decide when it will be best for you to address it. Timing is important when you're dealing with difficult people and situations.

Alexa, a high school science teacher, was struggling with the disruptive behavior of one of her students. One afternoon, after this student made a disrespectful comment, Alexa finally decided that she'd had enough. In front of the entire class, she impulsively launched into a loud, bitter, profanity-laced scolding of this student. The result was a formal reprimand from her supervisor. As another consequence, many of the other students and their parents lost confidence in Alexa's ability to manage her classroom. Alexa would have done better not to react in the moment and instead to confront the problem at another time, after cooling off and consulting with her co-workers about how to deal with this specific student.

How to Confront?

Can you think about confronting an unpleasant person or situation in a way that will lead to improvement? If it seems unlikely that the problem can be resolved, the best solution may be to know how to let it go. You will also be well served by knowing how to use methods of relaxation and mindfulness if you're caught up with an annoying person or stuck in an annoying situation, and how to assertively let someone know you're angry in a way that will improve communication rather than escalate conflict.

The Practice of Avoidance

Some of your anger probably arises in response to known, predictable triggers. For example, you may become angry when your children repeatedly resist doing their homework, when your spouse persists in asking the same accusatory questions, or when a co-worker approaches you again and again for favors. If you can arrange to be absent at times when you're likely to experience such triggers, you'll decrease your chances of becoming angry. The anger cycle will be delayed, and you can deal with the problem later.

Avoidance sometimes produces a degree of worry or guilt, but the trade-off is that anger can be temporarily avoided.

Steven, a fifty-two-year-old elementary school teacher, was married and had two children. He had no brothers or sisters. His father had died ten years earlier, and his eighty-two-year-old mother lived nearby in a small apartment.

The process of aging had taken its toll on Steven's mother. She was hard of hearing, a problem that made telephone conversations difficult, and her declining vision made it impossible for her to drive. Her ability to think clearly had also declined. In conversations, she would often forget what Steven had just said.

Because of all these issues, Steven's mother had become highly dependent on him. She called him at least twice a day. He had to drive her to the supermarket, pay her bills, repair small items in her apartment or hire contractors to make larger repairs, remind her of the children's birthdays, and take her to the doctor and the dentist. And her memory loss didn't help. Sometimes she called him at inconvenient times and said, "I forgot to tell you that I have to see the dentist this morning. Will you drive me?" or "I know we just went to the supermarket, but I forgot to buy ketchup. Will you please go and get it for me?" She often mailed checks for bills that Steven had already paid, and she regularly called him at work and insisted that he leave his classroom to talk with her.

The school principal tolerated these disruptions for a while, but eventually she told Steven to fix the problem. Friction was also developing between Steven and his wife, who felt neglected and complained that Steven wasn't spending enough time with their children, even though he frequently coached their sports teams.

Steven had frequent but unproductive arguments with his mother. He told her not to call him at work anymore. He insisted that she get a hearing aid, and he required her to make a shopping list before he would take her out. But she continued to forget much of what he told her, and his anger simmered.

Steven knew that he had to develop a long-term plan for his mother's care. In the meantime, he decided to use the practices of avoidance and escape to relieve some of the pressure. He posted a calendar on his mother's refrigerator door along with a sign indicating that he was unavailable Monday through Friday from eight in the morning until four in the afternoon. He also listed the days and times when he was unavailable because of coaching. He told his mother that they could talk on the phone only once a day, at about seven in the evening, and he no longer accepted her calls when she phoned him at work. To avoid unproductive arguments, he made it clear that he would stay for only *forty-five minutes when he visited her. In addition, he bought her an alarm to be worn around her neck in case she had to call emergency services.*

Initially Steven felt some guilt about avoiding his mother's phone calls, but he knew she would be safe until he could find a better situation for her. Once a plan for her care was put in place, he noticed improvement in his relationships with his wife and children, and he was more focused and productive at work. Eventually he moved his mother into a local facility where she could be looked after full time.

The practice of avoidance is not a cure-all, and it doesn't produce long-lasting results. It may even make a problem worse if the avoidance isn't explained. For example, if you decide not to attend your friend Mitchell's barbeque because Gary will be there and you always argue with him, it's best to tell Mitchell why you aren't going. But avoidance does buy you time to learn strategies for long-term anger management. It's a basic first step because it gives you an opportunity to rethink a problem and handle it in a better way. In some cases, avoidance may be the best (if temporary) solution to an immediate challenge you're facing. Of course, sometimes avoidance is impossible. But when you can practice avoidance thoughtfully, it can go a long way toward helping you prevent an outburst of anger.

Planned Avoidance

If you can identify a situation that has led you to become angry in the past, you can decide to avoid it in the future. For example, to avoid waiting too long at your doctor's office, you can arrange to be her first patient of the day. If you become angry when you arrive home from work and see your children's toys scattered all over the house, you can call when you're about to leave work so there will be time for your spouse, the nanny, or the children themselves to tidy up. To avoid the triggers of rush hour, you can ask your employer to let you change your work hours, work from home some of the time, or transfer to a branch in a less congested area. These examples may not apply to your situation, but almost everyone can occasionally avoid a dinner engagement when an angry blowup is likely. And sometimes an argument can be avoided if you can stay away from certain questions.

- Who did you go out with last night?

- Do you plan to have your son Bar Mitzvahed?

- What's the best church in town?

- Don't you think the Democrats [Republicans] are complete morons?

Allison and her husband lived across the country from his parents. At first when she and her husband would visit his family, they stayed for five or six days.

A predictable pattern emerged. The first two days were usually enjoyable. By the third or fourth day, tension would be building between Allison and her mother-in-law. The visits always ended on an unpleasant note.

After considering this pattern, Allison decided that it would be best if she and her husband limited their visits to three days. That way, she reasoned, their time with his parents would have a better chance of being enjoyable, and angry blowups would be less likely.

Avoidance via Delay

Suppose you're feeling put upon because someone you don't even like has asked you to do something that will be difficult or inconvenient and will require a major commitment of your time, such as serving on the board of a religious organization, driving an acquaintance to an appointment for a root canal, or watching a neighbor's pet while she goes on vacation. In situations like these, you can usually say, "Can I get back to you in a day or two?" The delay enables you to gain composure, consider more options, and develop a calmer and more reasonable response than might be forthcoming if you were to give your answer on the spot. Similarly, when a disruptive student voices a strong opinion that isn't relevant to the lesson at hand, a classroom teacher might say, "Let me think about what you're saying until tomorrow. I'll get back to you then." And when an aggressive reporter poses an uncomfortable question to a politician's press secretary, the press secretary might say, "I'll check on that for you." A simple delay can often defuse a situation.

Avoidance via Indirect Response

Many people think they have to confront a difficult situation with a direct, face-to-face response. With some thought, however, it's possible to respond more creatively and more productively by not responding directly and in the moment. For example, if your young son has broken a rule, and if your spouse is usually calm and constructive with him, then maybe it's better to let your spouse be the messenger and speak to your son about the problem. Or you may be able to avoid direct contact with your angry employee or co-worker by sending a thoughtful email or memo instead of dealing in person with a situation that is likely to trigger your anger. And if your spouse or partner triggers your anger at breakfast, you can send a text from work that expresses your ideas better than you could have done if you had responded in the heat of the moment (but, obviously, a text can also be angry, impulsive, and destructive, and so it should not be sent until your anger has subsided).

The Practice of Escape

Some situations just can't be avoided. You may have to lead a difficult meeting or attend a family function or show up in the bleachers for your child's base-ball game. If you're dealing with one of these situations, it's wise to think of some ways you can remove yourself if you should begin to feel angry.

Take a Time-Out

Sometimes it's best to walk away from a disagreement. As your anger builds, continued discussion may become unproductive and even damaging. For example, you can take a break and tell your teenager, "I'm upset now. Let's go out to eat. We can try to solve this problem later." Or when a con-versation with your spouse or partner becomes too heated, you can say, "I don't like where this is headed right now. Why don't we each take the rest of the afternoon to think, and we can try again to talk this through later tonight?" And when a conflict comes up during a phone call, it's even easier to say, "We probably shouldn't continue this right now. I'll call you back tonight."

A time-out from conflict requires thoughtful action on your part, and leaving a situation when your anger starts to build can be a good way to interrupt the anger cycle and develop better control. The basic idea is to identify a situation in which you typically become angry with someone and usually end up in a big argument, and then practice getting away (for example, by going out for a walk to cool down) after you've noticed yourself becoming angry.

In teaching people to use time-outs effectively, we've found that it's helpful for them to take the following three steps. Practicing these steps will break up your usual pattern of making negative comments and give you a sense of success as well as better self-control:

1. When you see that you're becoming angry during a specific conversation, notice when you say something negative in anger. *That will be your signal to calmly remove yourself from the conversation.* Just leave! It may take some practice for you to become aware of your reactions and stop an angry conversation.

2. Observe your own general internal experience of anger, and practice leaving more situations before you say anything negative. As you notice your anger building, don't say anything at all—again, just leave!

3. Work on more elegant exits. Before removing yourself from the conversation, tell the other person that you're becoming angry, that you're going to leave, and that you'd like to try to resolve the issue at a later time. Here, it's important for you to actually follow up and attempt a resolution.

Plan Your Escape

It may be difficult for you to just get up and leave a situation when your presence is expected. But if you had realized in advance that dealing with a particular person was likely to get you angry, wouldn't you have placed a limit on the time you were willing to spend with him or her? After all, why put time and energy into unproductive, contentious dialogue? It's always unhelpful.

If you know you're headed into a problematic interaction, you can say up front that you have time constraints: "I'm happy we can talk about this. But I want you to know that I only have half an hour before I have to see a client." This doesn't mean that you should lie. It means that you can organize your schedule in a way that automatically puts a time limit on a potentially difficult interaction.

Another possibility is to have someone help you get out of a situation that's likely to be unpleasant and lead to anger. For example, you might ask your assistant to interrupt a meeting after thirty minutes and remind you about your next appointment. To use the practice of escape successfully, you need to anticipate situations in which you're likely to become angry and then put a plan in place for an early exit.

Distract Yourself with an Enjoyable Activity

Thinking over and over again about a problem may increase your anger, and it doesn't usually produce a good solution, so there's a real place for distraction. It's also true, of course, that putting and keeping your head in the sand will probably increase your anger because some problems do get worse over time. In the short term, however, distracting yourself may be helpful.

What does it mean to distract yourself? It simply means becoming absorbed in a non-anger-related and, preferably, enjoyable activity. After an anger-filled workday, you can go to a bowling alley, a baseball game, a movie, or a restaurant with a family member, or you can have a phone conversation with an old friend. It's important that the anger-related situation not be discussed while you're distracting yourself, so if anger-related thoughts intrude during a recreational activity, let them pass and then bring your mental focus back to the activity at hand. The goal is to break the cycle of obsessing about whatever has led to your anger. What you do instead is focus on more positive thoughts and more pleasurable activities. At the most basic level, distraction is about creating more balance in your life by taking the time to engage in activities that you enjoy. (You'll find more tips for a happier life in chapter 15 of this book, downloadable from http://www.newharbinger.com/42266.)

Avoidance and Escape: Putting It All Together

Refer to practice exercise 5, and ask yourself whether there any anger triggers in your life that you can sidestep by means of avoidance. Can you use planned avoidance? Perhaps a delay? Possibly figure out a way to respond indirectly? Remember, avoidance is only a temporary solution intended to give you some distance from a problem until a more permanent solution can be found.

Now, referring again to practice exercise 5, think about something you have to do this week that may provoke your anger, but that you can't avoid. Can you take a time-out from this problematic obligation? (If so, remember the three steps of an effective time-out.) Maybe plan your escape? Perhaps engage in a pleasant distraction after the situation has passed? Again, remember that escape, like avoidance, is a temporary solution on the way to a longer-term plan for managing anger.

Key Points

☑ Not every problematic person or situation needs to be immediately confronted. Choosing your battles—that is, learning to recognize *which* people and situations are worth dealing with and *which* to let go, and then deciding *when* and *how* to engage with the ones you've chosen to deal with—will help you sidestep provocations and manage your life with less anger.

☑ "Avoidance" means anticipating a problem and keeping away from a person or a situation likely to trigger your anger.

☑ "Escape" means removing yourself from a person or a situation after you've noticed that your anger is building.

☑ Avoidance and escape by themselves aren't enough. They don't allow for meaningful personal growth, and in the long term they're not helpful with situations that grow worse over time. But avoidance and escape are simple first steps that you can take when you find yourself in an actual or potentially angry interaction.

☑ By practicing avoidance or escape in problematic situations, you'll get better at temporarily sidestepping life's difficulties.

CHAPTER 6

Strategy Three:
Find New Solutions to Social Problems

The way to cope with the future is to create it.

—Dennis Gabor

* Everyone faces challenges. Struggles are a part of life, and dealing with them is one way for human beings to grow. Even if it were possible to live without difficulties and conflicts, such a life would cause intellectual and emotional stagnation. Nevertheless, some people seem to believe that a state of bliss—a life without hassles—is possible and even good. Then, when problems inevitably come up anyway, these people get bent out of shape. We see such people's vision of life as unrealistic. True personal development, we believe, is achieved when a person can look calmly at a problem, hunt for a reasonable (if imperfect) solution, and grow through the process of finding that solution.

You've probably noticed, however, that not everybody becomes wiser with age. Some people grow from their misfortunes; others don't. Those who don't are often stuck in their anger (see "Getting Stuck in Anger"). They complain, remain unhappy, and often wind up being rejected by others. Your reactions to the struggles in your own life, whether those struggles are big or

* *Before you begin this chapter, we recommend that you download practice exercise 6 (Solving Social Problems) from http://www.newharbinger.com/42266.*

small, have consequences. On the one hand, if you look at problems as challenges to be met, and if you minimize your anger while working on those challenges, it's likely that you'll have satisfying results. On the other hand, if you scream and yell, pout and throw things, and close your mind to suggestions, it's unlikely that you'll have desirable results.

Learning how to react constructively to difficult people and situations requires personal awareness and a willingness to explore new approaches. In many ways, how you approach problems sets the stage for your life to improve, get worse, or stay the same. People who develop wisdom remain relatively unflustered, remember lessons from the past, and use those lessons to determine which responses to future problems will bring about good results—and which won't.

In our professional work, we've met a lot of people who weren't aware of the consequences of their actions. They approached problems by obsessing about what they saw as unfair and unjust treatment at the hands of others. They complained and whined about unusual frustrations, but also about those that were ordinary. They contemplated revenge and fantasized about it. They pouted and shouted. They used a variety of harmful avoidance activities, such as drinking, excessive gambling, and substance use. They stayed away from home, from school, and from family members for long periods. Obviously, such reactions don't lead to successful problem solving.

We can't give you advice for tackling the specific problems you're facing. You know your struggles best, and you're ultimately responsible for your choices. But what we can do in this chapter is teach you a technique known as *social problem solving*, in which you come up with a menu of options for solving a problem, pick the best option from that menu, and learn and grow as you make your choices.

And we do think you have choices. How you react to difficulties over the long term will affect the quality of your life, and we want to help you achieve the best, most satisfying life you can. We hope you'll be able both to reduce your anger and to develop more constructive solutions to the challenges you face.

Getting Stuck in Anger

One downside of anger is that people tend to get caught up in it. As a result, they don't pay attention to the most basic questions: *Is what I'm doing working? Is it effective? Am I getting what I want?* Consider how you would answer the questions associated with the following life situations:

- *Marriage:* What happens when I yell at my wife? Does she feel better? Do I feel better? Do we grow closer? What can I do to actually solve our problems?

- *Work:* What happens when I argue with my co-workers? Am I seen as an effective employee? Does our work improve? What could I do to resolve our conflicts and create a better and more productive workplace?

- *Driving:* What happens when I curse at other drivers on the road and tailgate them? Do they become better drivers?

- *Parenting:* What happens when I yell "No!" as my children are nagging me? Do they feel better? Do I feel better? Do we grow closer? How can I help them get what they want while keeping them safe and creating a minimum of discomfort for myself?

Styles of Social Problem Solving

If you're like most people, you've probably developed a consistent approach to the way you face difficulties. Over time, this approach has become a pattern that's part of your personality. Psychological research shows that most people have one of three styles for solving social problems, two of them negative and one of them positive:

1. An *impulsive, careless* style

2. An *avoidant* style

3. A *positive* style[19]

Which one of these three do *you* use to tackle life's difficulties?

Negative Problem Solving: Impulsiveness and Avoidance

People who use negative problem solving see life's challenges as threatening and overwhelming. They have little confidence in their ability to find solutions. They doubt their skills. They say such things to themselves as "It's too hard. There's nothing I can do. This problem can't be solved. There's just no answer." Their pessimistic viewpoint limits their search for solutions, and their results are likely to be poor.

Negative problem solving is characterized by two of the styles just listed: an impulsive, careless style and an avoidant style. Both are bad, and if you use either of them, it's important that you change your pattern. We explained in chapter 5 that in order to minimize anger, it's sometimes wise to temporarily avoid a problematic situation or person. Knowing which situations to avoid, and which to face, is an important key to negotiating the difficulties of life. As we hope we've made clear, however, avoidance is acceptable only in the short term. It is not a good long-term practice when it comes to dealing with major life issues. Over time, avoidance can compound some problems and lead to more frustration, worry, and anger. The stories of Mark and Marjorie highlight the cumulative effects of both the impulsive style (Mark's) and the avoidant style (Marjorie's) of facing life's challenges.

Mark, a thirty-two-year-old carpenter, experienced strong anger reactions that had been causing problems for most of his adult life. A particular area of concern was his anger while he was driving. He would speed up, tailgate, and yell obscenities at drivers who cut him off or drove too slowly. He did this impulsively, without thinking about the possible results.

In one serious incident, Mark followed a car that had cut him off until he pushed it off the road. After both cars had come to a stop on the shoulder, Mark jumped out to tell the other driver off. But as Mark approached the other car, its driver threatened him with a gun.

This incident shook Mark, but he didn't change his behavior. In fact, he was later arrested several times for reckless driving and eventually lost his license. After each of his arrests, Mark claimed that he regretted his behavior, but it continued, to the point where he even drove for some months without a license. On the road, in the heat of the moment, he rarely considered his options for dealing with other drivers who were rude. For Mark, there was only one possible course of action—confrontation.

Mark had similar difficulties at work. Although he had a good work ethic, he was unable to handle disagreements. For example, in response to minor criticism from his supervisor or one of his fellow employees, Mark would impulsively deliver a long, angry speech, criticize the critic, and occasionally engage in a shoving match. And if a customer complained about his work, Mark ignored the criticism and immediately labeled the customer as picky, spoiled, and impossible to please. In addition, he sometimes damaged property by acting with intentional carelessness.

Mark's anger-driven, impulsive pattern of reacting showed itself almost every day. Over time, these angry reactions damaged his personal relationships, derailed his career, and created a host of additional frustrations that he had to deal with.

Marjorie, a bright and outgoing thirty-eight-year-old counselor, worked at a nonprofit agency. Recently divorced, she had two children, six and eight years old. She also had a good deal of financial stress, which contributed to an ongoing struggle with her ex-husband, who was not consistently paying the agreed-upon child support.

Marjorie was having problems at work, too. She didn't get along with her immediate supervisor and had been overlooked for promotions that she thought she deserved.

On the surface, Marjorie appeared to possess the personal strengths needed to cope with life's pressures. But she rarely faced her problems directly. She avoided seeing people with whom she thought she might get into a conflict and simply hoped that things would take care of themselves. For example, instead of hiring a lawyer to enforce her husband's agreement to pay child support, she put off meeting with an attorney and hoped her ex-husband would comply on his own. And instead of looking for another job, she waited in silence, hoping that her supervisor would leave.

Because of her inaction, Marjorie's difficulties grew worse. And as her problems piled up and intensified, she found herself increasingly overwhelmed.

Over time, her life became chaotic. But when Marjorie was asked what she planned to do about the chaos in her life, she just said, "Lots of people are in situations like mine. I doubt there's any real solution." Feelings of anger, bitterness, and sadness dominated her daily life.

It's easy to see the effects that Mark's and Marjorie's patterns of social problem solving had on their lives. If you, like Mark and Marjorie, have a negative style of social problem solving, there's still some good news—with effort, you can change the way you make decisions and how you respond to the unavoidable hassles of life.

Positive Problem Solving

People who see life's problems as challenges to be met have adopted a positive style of solving social problems. These people are generally optimistic, patient, and committed to getting the results they want. They have a thoughtful, careful approach to life and make decisions that aren't ruled by anger.

Bernie, a retired car salesperson in his late sixties, was cheerful, outgoing, and intelligent. But he'd had his share of difficulties and struggles over the course of his life.

At the age of twenty-four, he married his high school sweetheart, and the couple was very happy. But when Bernie was in his early thirties, his wife died unexpectedly, leaving him with three children to care for.

Within three years Bernie remarried, this time to a woman from the automobile dealership where he worked. His second marriage ended in divorce, but not before another child was born.

During his working years, Bernie had spent most of his income providing for his children. He also had the usual ups and downs that go along with childrearing, managing a household, and advancing a career.

By his fifties, Bernie had developed a certain grace under pressure. When he faced a difficulty, he was able to draw on his childlike curiosity, which helped him find the one solution that would provide the best results. For the most part, he chose not to react to problems immediately or emotionally. Instead, he would take a step back, a temporary approach that often allowed him to put his energy into gathering information at the library or online, or asking trusted friends how they might handle the situation in question.

Bernie was always in a state of learning and growth. Each of his struggles opened up a new opportunity for him to develop skills and knowledge. He usually found a creative way to navigate challenges, and he almost never made a difficult situation worse.

All four of Bernie's children eventually graduated from high school with good grades, and all four went to local universities. One is now an accountant, one is a teacher, another is a stay-at-home mom, and the youngest followed Bernie's career path and works in the automobile industry. And Bernie, over the years, because of his approach to problems, became someone others frequently sought out for advice.

The Six Steps of Social Problem Solving

Just as an anger episode analysis is concerned with six components (a trigger, thoughts, experience, an action urge, anger expression, and outcomes; see chapter 2), the process of social problem solving has six steps:

1. Clearly identify the problem

2. Identify potential solutions

3. Identify likely short-term outcomes of your potential solutions

4. Identify likely long-term outcomes of your potential solutions

5. Select the best solution and put it into practice

6. Evaluate your solution

In your daily life, you can refer to practice exercise 6 as a guide to the steps of social problem solving. Throughout this chapter we'll use the example of Billy to illustrate the first four steps.

Lots of Yelling, No End in Sight

Billy, a thirty-year-old welder, was having frequent arguments with his wife. When he first came to us for individual counseling, Billy was fuming.

"My wife—I think she's crazy," he said. "All she does is yell; so naturally I yell back. She acts this way all the time. I don't know what to do. Damn!"

Billy kept on this way for a while, but without giving us any detailed examples of what he meant.

Step 1. Clearly Identify the Problem

When you identify an ongoing social problem, what you're actually doing is naming one of your anger triggers (see chapter 2). To identify a trigger clearly, concretely, and objectively, you can use what we call the *when-then* format, with *when* followed by a description of the problematic situation, and *then* followed by a description of how you reacted. Using this format helps you begin to focus on the problem and move on to understanding your personal reactions. It also allows you to relate what happened without excess descriptive baggage, such as casting blame or exaggerating the situation and its importance.

In using the *when-then* format, it's important that you identify only one problem at a time. This means that each problem you identify will require you to start again from the first part of step 1. It isn't always easy to state a problem in the *when-then* format, but if you give it some thought, you will always be able to do it.

For example, let's say your problem is continuing and unwelcome contact with your ex-husband, who keeps calling to harass you and argue with you. You could identify the problem by saying, "I want my ex-husband to stop calling me," but that statement isn't specific enough for you to work with. Instead, reformulate the problem this way: "*When* my ex-husband calls and says rude things, *then* we argue, and I become angry, and *then* I think this misery will never end, and I feel lousy for the rest of the day." Figure 6.1 shows Billy's statement of his problem in the *when-then* format.

Step 1. Clearly Identify the Problem

Using the *when-then* format, describe a problem. Include what you did, how someone else reacted, what each of you said, and what you thought.

When...

After a hard day at work, I stopped off for a drink with my friends. I knew my wife had cooked dinner, but I forgot to call and tell her I'd be late. She was frowning when I got home. She said, "Where the hell have you been? I've been waiting for almost an hour, and now dinner is ruined."

Then...

I think she didn't understand that I'd had major problems at work and needed to be with my friends for a while. So I told her that, and we went back and forth, arguing and yelling. Finally, I said, "Just shut up." Then I went down to the basement to watch TV, and she went to bed.

Figure 6.1. Billy's Responses to Step 1 of Practice Exercise 6

Step 2. Identify Potential Solutions

Step 2 is to come up with a number of potential solutions—several options, reactions, or paths that are available to you as you attempt to deal with your problem. The goal is to develop a *range* of potential solutions—a menu of options, so to speak.

One aspect of this approach is to think differently about problems and identify possible courses of action that you wouldn't normally consider. At first you may find yourself going toward an extreme solution. You may say, for example, "When my ex-husband calls, I can notify the police and tell them I want a restraining order against him." That kind of extreme potential solution is common, and it's perfectly normal. When you're angry, you'll often find yourself thinking in narrow and distorted ways. But once you begin to imagine all the other available alternatives, it becomes easier for you to see more effective solutions. So if all you're coming up with is a set of solutions that seem likely to make your problem worse, just continue thinking of other possibilities.

With persistence, you'll eventually come up with several constructive alternatives, and the whole process will become easier as you continue to use it. In the meantime, go ahead and generate a range of alternatives, from those that are likely to be wholly ineffective to those that you can actually use. How many potential solutions you identify will depend on your problem, on how creative you are, and on how much you practice. We recommend that you try to come up with at least five potential solutions, but if you can come up with more, that's even better. Figure 6.2 shows Billy's list of potential solutions to the problem he identified.

Step 2. Identify Potential Solutions

List at least five possible solutions to the problem you identified in step 1.

1. Tell her I'm stressed out, I'm still hungry, and I don't have to answer to her.

2. Avoid her—leave the house and go drinking.

3. Tell her she's just like her mother.

4. Stop and get her flowers before I come home.

5. Apologize and ask her what to do in the future.

Figure 6.2. Billy's Responses to Step 2 of Practice Exercise 6

Step 3. Identify Likely Short-Term Outcomes

Short-term outcomes are the immediate reactions you're likely to get from others. Be aware, however, that focusing only on immediate outcomes can be a mistake. For example, if you're angry and yell at your son for fighting with his sister, you may get your son's immediate compliance. Over the long term however, yelling at your son will probably create emotional distance in your relationship and model bad behavior for him.

Even if a likely short-term outcome isn't completely clear, you can usually make an educated guess about what will happen if you take a particular course of action. The goal is to come up with the *most* likely outcome. Figure 6.3 shows Billy's list of likely short-term outcomes for the potential solutions he identified.

Step 3. Identify Likely Short-Term Outcomes of Your Potential Solutions

List the likely short-term outcomes of the potential solutions you identified in step 2.

1. *We eat dinner in bitter silence.*

2. *She becomes very angry, then worried.*

3. *More arguing. She tells me I'm selfish.*

4. *She's both angry and happy.*

5. *She vents a bit, then gives me suggestions. I listen. Some sound OK, some don't.*

Figure 6.3. Billy's Responses to Step 3 of Practice Exercise 6

Step 4. Identify Likely Long-Term Outcomes

Long-term outcomes are those that unfold over time—hours, days, months, even years. For example, hitting people or causing property damage to teach them a lesson may feel good in the moment. Yet in the long term this kind of behavior may bring time-consuming, disruptive, costly problems with the law.

Again, if a likely long-term outcome isn't immediately clear to you, make an educated guess about the *most* likely outcome. Figure 6.4 shows Billy's list of likely long-term outcomes for the potential solutions he identified.

Step 4. Identify Likely Long-Term Outcomes of Your Potential Solutions

List the likely long-term outcomes of the potential solutions you identified in step 2.

1. *Lack of open communication; ongoing bitterness.*

2. *We don't talk for days. She's quietly uncooperative.*

3. *We never work this situation out.*

4. *She feels temporarily better until it happens again.*

5. *Together, we develop a plan and agree what to do in the future.*

Figure 6.4. Billy's Responses to Step 4 of Practice Exercise 6

Step 5. Select the Best Solution and Put It into Practice

As you consider the likely short- and long-term outcomes of each potential solution, don't rule out any solution until you've gone through your entire menu of options. Then start the selection process by eliminating potential solutions that are unlikely to lead to desirable outcomes. For example, take another look at figure 6.2, which shows Billy's responses to step 2 of practice exercise 6. Solutions 1, 2, and 3 (stonewalling, avoiding his wife, telling her she's just like her mother) aren't likely to be effective, but solutions 4 and 5 (getting her flowers, apologizing) may be worthwhile, since these solutions can reduce conflict in the short run and strengthen the relationship over time. You will usually come up with two or three solutions that may produce a good outcome. Your task is to pick one of those good options. For Billy, an apology is likely to be the best solution in terms of its long-term outcome (but see "A Word About Apologies").

Be realistic while you're working toward selecting the best solution. Consider the skills you'll need in order to take any specific course of action.

Otherwise you may make the common mistake of choosing a solution that you don't have the skills to implement, even though that solution would be likely to produce the most positive outcome.

Ronald, a cook, was unhappy about his salary. He thought at first that his best option would be to directly ask his boss for a raise and agree to take on more responsibility. But that strategy was risky because Ronald didn't possess the skills to create a better menu or respond to his boss's criticisms of his work performance. Taking the time needed to become a more accomplished cook, and to learn the skills of successfully negotiating a raise, might have been a good long-term approach for Ronald. He also could have sought coaching to help him respond productively to criticism. For the time being, however, a more realistic option for Ronald was to update his résumé and see whether other employers were offering more money.

A Word About Apologies

Offering an apology can be difficult, especially when anger is involved. If you're feeling mistreated, neglected, disrespected, or otherwise harmed, you may very well wonder why *you* should be the one to apologize. That's certainly an understandable position, especially because when you're angry you usually also feel some moral indignation about who was right and who was wrong in a particular interaction or situation. Nevertheless, an apology can often set the stage for resolving a problem.

Let's say, for example, that you were truly wrong for coming home late and not calling first. In this situation you might say, "I want to apologize for my behavior. I was wrong and I'm sorry. I'll try to do better in the future." But there are also lots of situations in which you don't think you were wrong and in which you'd be foolish to accept all the blame. In those situations, you might focus on the larger problem: "I'm sorry that our relationship has reached this point. I don't like what you did, but I understand that I also played a part in what happened. I'm sorry about the whole thing and hope we can move forward and find a solution."

This specific example and these particular responses may not fit your situation exactly. But you get the point. If you start with a statement of regret, even mild regret, that statement can go a long way toward helping you find an effective resolution.

Step 6. Evaluate Your Solution

Once you've decided on a solution—one you believe you have the necessary skills to implement—you're ready to evaluate it (that is, observe what happens when you put your solution into practice). As mentioned earlier, the greater your awareness of how your actions and reactions influence others, the more that awareness will contribute to your overall growth and effectiveness.

Get Support—and Open Your Mind

When you're just starting to use this new and different way of solving problems, you may find it helpful to work with a trusted friend, a family member, or a counselor. (In our own personal lives, we too consult with friends about difficult problems before we choose a course of action.) Consider using practice exercise 6 on one or two problems each week, until the six-step process becomes more automatic for you. Figure 6.5, at the end of this chapter, shows Billy's responses to practice exercise 6.

We have found the six-step process described in this chapter to be among the most practical ways of managing anger. You can use this process for a variety of problems and in a wide range of situations. The key is to open your mind and allow yourself to think about your problems in a different way. As you do, you'll become more and more capable of creating solutions that are effective not just in the moment but also, very often, over the long term.

Key Points

☑ How you approach social problems sets the stage for conditions in your life to improve, get worse, or stay the same.

☑ Negative social problem solving is characterized by impulsive decisions, responses made in anger, avoidance, and the hope that problems will solve themselves.

☑ Positive social problem solving is characterized by an optimistic, patient, careful approach to facing difficulties, and it includes seeing problems as challenges to be met.

☑ The six-step approach to solving social problems can be applied to a wide range of situations and can help you find constructive solutions to the problems you face. The steps of social problem solving are to clearly identify the problem and come up with potential solutions (that is, outline the problem in concrete terms and generate a menu of options, which you do in steps 1 and 2); to assess the probable outcomes of each potential solution (that is, to consider both short and long-term outcomes, which you do in steps 3 and 4); to select the best solution and put it into practice (that is, pick the best course of action from that menu, which you do in step 5); and to evaluate your solution (that is, learn and grow as you make your choices, which you do in step 6).

Step 1. Clearly Identify the Problem

Using the *when-then* format, describe a problem. Include what you did, how someone else reacted, what each of you said, and what you thought.

When...

After a hard day at work, I stopped off for a drink with my friends. I knew my wife had cooked dinner, but I forgot to call and tell her I'd be late. She was frowning when I got home. She said, "Where the hell have you been? I've been waiting for almost an hour, and now dinner is ruined."

Then...

I think she didn't understand that I'd had major problems at work and needed to be with my friends for a while. So I told her that, and we want back and forth, arguing and yelling. Finally, I said, "Just shut up." Then I went down to the basement to watch TV, and she went to bed.

Step 2. Identify Potential Solutions

List at least five possible solutions to the problem you identified in step 1.

1. Tell her I'm stressed out, I'm still hungry, and I don't have to answer to her.

2. Avoid her—leave the house and go drinking.

3. Tell her she's just like her mother.

4. Stop and get her flowers before I come home.

5. Apologize and ask her what to do in the future.

Figure 6.5. Billy's Completed Exercise for Solving Social Problems

Step 3. Identify Likely Short-Term Outcomes of Your Potential Solutions

List the likely short-term outcomes of the potential solutions you identified in step 2.

1. *We eat dinner in bitter silence.*

2. *She becomes very angry, then worried.*

3. *More arguing. She tells me I'm selfish.*

4. *She's both angry and happy.*

5. *She vents a bit, then gives me suggestions. I listen. Some sound OK, some don't.*

Step 4. Identify Likely Long-Term Outcomes of Your Potential Solutions

List the likely long-term outcomes of the potential solutions you identified in step 2.

1. *Lack of open communication; ongoing bitterness.*

2. *We don't talk for days. She's quietly uncooperative.*

3. *We never work this situation out.*

4. *She feels temporarily better until it happens again.*

5. *Together, we develop a plan and agree what to do in the future.*

Figure 6.5. continued

PART 3

Changing Thoughts
That Lead to Anger

CHAPTER 7

Strategy Four:
Change the Way You Think About Your Life

We can complain because rose bushes have thorns or rejoice because thorn bushes have roses.

—Alphonse Karr

* Problems are a part of life. No matter how much you work to develop effective skills for dealing with difficult situations, or how hard you try to stay calm in the face of misfortune, you can bet that life will continue to present you with new and unexpected challenges—a lost job, an illness, trouble in your marriage, others' foolish behavior, gossip directed against you, unfairness at work or at school, and so on. For this reason, it's important that you develop ways of thinking realistically about misfortune and understanding it for what it is—an unpleasant inconvenience. The overwhelming majority of your anger triggers, regardless of how horrible they seem in the moment, cause little more than lost time, dignity, or money. These situations are social in nature. They aren't life-threatening, and that's why we call them inconveniences.

This chapter introduces you to six irrational thought patterns and six ways to think differently and intelligently about struggles and misfortune so

* Before you begin this chapter, we recommend that you download practice exercise 7 (Think Differently and Better in Anger Situations) and practice exercise 2 (Anger Episode Record) from http://www .newharbinger.com/42266.

that your anger can be lessened. The approach you'll learn is very simple, but it isn't easy. In order to think differently about the difficult aspects of your life, it is important that you develop awareness of your irrational thoughts, and that you find the time to practice using alternative thoughts. The goal is to bring about a shift in how you view the world so that you react less strongly to daily hassles and inconveniences.

Your Thinking Creates Your Anger

Like every other human being, you're a thinking creature. In other words, you're constantly sensing, observing, interpreting, evaluating, and making judgments about events in your life, not just reacting to them. The way you think about events has a powerful influence on your feelings and actions. Your thinking contributes to your anger and to some of the self-defeating behavior that goes along with anger. Over time, like everyone else, you've developed patterns of thought, and years of repetition have made these patterns automatic and inflexible.

And, like almost everyone else, you're probably unaware of how you are thinking when an anger trigger appears. After all, your thinking patterns and the thoughts that arise from them seem perfectly normal to you because you've been using these patterns and thinking these thoughts for many years. Becoming more aware of how you typically think when you become angry, and changing your long-standing thoughts, are of key importance in reducing your anger. You'll need to put some effort and practice into changing the way you think about unpleasant events, but the good news is that effort and practice will reduce your anger and increase your joy and happiness.

Do you believe that other people cause your anger with their disagreeable and otherwise unwanted behavior? If so, you're making what we referred to in chapter 2 as the *big mistake*. But the truth is that *you are in charge of how you think*, and this means that you have more control over your anger than you realize.

For example, imagine you're on a busy highway when another driver suddenly swerves into your lane. You hit the brakes and give a warning honk, only to have him honk back in anger and give you the finger. Obviously, you might have a range of reactions to this scenario. Would any of the following eight thoughts lead you to feel little or no anger?

1. This guy is an ass who deserves to be taught a lesson.

2. I don't know anything about this person. Maybe he wasn't paying attention. I'll let it go.

3. Who does he think he is? I'm not going to take this crap. I'll show him I'm not intimidated.

4. I'm getting too old to react to this kind of stuff. I can stay calm and in control.

5. He shouldn't be acting this way. He's being completely unfair, since he's the one who wasn't paying attention.

6. It would be nice if all drivers were fair and considerate, but some aren't. That's just the way the world is.

7. What he's doing is terrible. I'm not going to stand for it.

8. This isn't a big deal. I don't have to react.

You probably can see that thoughts 2, 4, 6, and 8 are likely to lead to the least anger.

How do people develop thinking responses that allow them to easily let go of their anger? Cognitive behavioral therapists like Albert Ellis and Aaron Beck have contributed to the development of four steps that can help you reevaluate and change how you think.[20]

Step 1. Become Aware of and Skeptical About Your Thinking

Two tendencies will make it difficult for you to change your thinking:

1. The tendency to be unaware of what you think

2. The tendency to assume that what you think is true

Being Unaware of What You Think

Most of us are unaware of our thoughts. If we try to tune in to the flow of our thoughts in real time, we notice that, moment by moment, the mind is busy dealing with a vast amount of information.

Our thoughts are always with us. They're part of our daily existence, and so we probably don't spend much time being aware of them. Like the air around us, which is crucial to our survival, our thoughts are crucial to the development and reduction of our anger. But just as we don't spend much time thinking about air, we don't spend much time taking an outsider's perspective on our thoughts.

Try this experiment. Put this book down, and spend thirty seconds sitting quietly and observing what's going on in your mind. You'll notice that thoughts come and go, and that your mind drifts. Notice how you're constantly judging, evaluating, and predicting your experience.

Now recall the last time you were angry. Do you remember what was going through your mind or what you were telling yourself? Put this book down once again and, in your mind, complete the following sentence: "The last time I was angry, I thought..."

You may notice that some of your thoughts are easy for you to find and report. For example, what are you thinking right now as you read the words on this page? With minimal effort, you can access your thoughts in the here and now just by focusing on them. Other thoughts are fleeting and operate below the level of your conscious awareness, often because they are connected to your deepest beliefs. But it's important for you to get in touch with those deeper thoughts because becoming more aware of how you think and evaluate situations when you're angry is a crucial first step toward improving your life.

Assuming That What You Think Is True

If you're like almost everybody else, you take your thoughts to be the truth. That means you're likely to have a high degree of confidence in what you're thinking. You believe that you're correctly interpreting events, the intentions of others, and the world around you, and that your judgments lead you to good decisions and healthy behavior. There's no question that your thoughts are real to you. But the truth is that your thoughts are mostly a product of your history and learning.

Let's look at Eli, Daniel, Kathy, and Wayne, all in their early twenties:

- Eli grew up with strict parents who had the attitude that children should do what they're told, with no back talk. There was also a strong sense of right and wrong in Eli's childhood home, and he learned that it's important to stand up for what is right, at all costs.

- Daniel grew up in a household that emphasized relationships and getting along with others. He was taught that it's sometimes necessary to consider the other person's perspective, even when you think you're right.

- Kathy was taught to be cautious in relationships. Trust, she was told, is something that others have to earn. She was brought up to believe that the most important thing is to be independent and strong.

- Wayne was treated harshly by his parents. He developed little self-confidence and was frequently worried that he wouldn't measure up to most other people's standards.

Each of these four individuals is in the early stages of a romantic relationship, and they have a problem in common—the people they're dating habitually show up forty-five minutes late for planned get-togethers. All four have thoughts about what this behavior means and what they should do about it. Using the little bit of historical information you have, see if you can correctly match each of the following thoughts with one of these four people:

1. My date isn't really that interested in me. I'm going to end things first, to show that I'm not needy.

2. This is bullcrap, and I'm not going to put up with lateness any longer.

3. It's probably my fault. It's probably because of something I said. I always mess these things up.

4. I don't like what's happening, and I want to find out what's behind it.

Here are the answers:

Kathy: 1

Eli: 2

Wayne: 3

Daniel: 4

Were you able to see how these individuals' different histories shaped how they think about their current experience?

Step 2. Identify What You Think When You Feel Angry

You, too, make a lot of evaluations about events in your everyday life, and to some extent these thoughts are guided by your previous experience. But your thoughts may not be accurate, realistic, or even helpful, especially when you're angry. As you become more aware of your thinking, it's important to begin seeing your thoughts for what they are—a private stream of evaluative words influenced by your personal history but not necessarily reflecting the truth.

One way to do this is to consult the following list of six irrational thought patterns as you recall several of your anger experiences, using the anger episodes you recorded in practice exercise 2 or using that exercise to analyze several different anger episodes as you move forward. (Psychologists call this a *self-monitoring task*.) While performing this task, keep in mind that the thoughts most immediately connected to an anger experience are the thoughts of interest. See if you can pinpoint the irrational patterns and thoughts that are most typical of what you're thinking during an anger episode:

1. *Awfulizing*: This is one of the worst things that could ever happen.

2. *Low frustration tolerance*: I can't handle this situation.

3. *Demandingness*: My family should be acting differently.

4. *Other-rating*: My colleague is a real jerk.

5. *Self-rating*: Deep down, I think I'm unimportant and not worthwhile.

6. *Distortion or misinterpretation*: My thinking is distorted, and I'm not seeing things clearly.

These six irrational patterns are important because they represent common errors in thinking that contribute to anger development. Dealing with such errors now will do a lot to help you manage your reactions more effectively in the future.

Awfulizing

Awfulizing is about exaggerating the consequences or the level of hardship associated with a difficult situation. Perhaps you describe daily hassles with words like "awful," "horrible," or "terrible" rather than "unfortunate," "bad," or "inconvenient." This is a problem because "awful," "terrible," and "horrible" are very strong words. When they're examined carefully, it's clear that their meaning is "All is lost." That phrase is appropriate for describing the devastation that follows an earthquake, a plane crash, a tornado, a hurricane, or the loss of life itself. But when these words are used in connection with an everyday frustration, setback, or hassle, they exaggerate the negative aspect of the situation. They're too strong to accurately describe what is taking place. When you characterize an ordinary challenge as "awful," "horrible," or "terrible," you reduce your motivation to face misfortune skillfully. You also stop yourself from coming up with an effective solution to whatever the problem is.

Low Frustration Tolerance

Low frustration tolerance is the tendency to underestimate your ability to deal with discomfort or misfortune. When a difficult or unfair situation comes up, the question that arises is often "Is this tolerable?" And it's pretty amazing how often people use the word "intolerable" to indicate their inability to deal with a problem. For example, you may say, "I can't stand it" when you're waiting in a long, slow-moving line, or "I'm at my wits' end" when your child spills juice on the rug, or "I can't deal with this crap anymore" when an expected promotion falls through. But these are ordinary setbacks and irritations. You will increase your anger if you see a simple misfortune as something that you cannot deal with. Low frustration tolerance will also distract you from coming up with an effective solution. In addition, whining and moaning about your inability to tolerate or cope with an unpleasant event will make you less pleasant to be around. The real meaning of "I can't stand it" is "I'm going to die." In fact, however, life is full of challenges, big and small, and most people who are betrayed, lose their jobs, fail in school, are rejected, and so on, do manage to adjust and adapt. Life moves on regardless of whether you think you can cope with it, so why not be optimistic, or at least realistic, about your skills and abilities?

Demandingness

Demandingness is the tendency to turn your personal preferences into inflexible, unbendable rules that you expect others and the world at large to follow. It's reflected in words and phrases like "they must," "you should," "he ought to," and "she has to," all of which suggest that there are no reasonable alternatives to what you happen to want. But others' behavior is determined by a variety of factors, such as human nature, imitation, learning history, and cultural norms. Therefore, when you are demanding, you ignore reality because you forget that the world is complex, and that conditions won't always support your getting everything you want.

It's true, of course, that some things in this world really must happen. We must eat, sleep, breathe, and so forth. But *must* your daughter go to college, even if she's very bright? *Must* your boss appreciate your hard work? *Must* your husband do what you ask? *Must* your children listen to your advice? *Must* your teachers recognize your creativity? *Must* your students realize how hard you worked on today's lesson plan? *Must* the gardener or the electrician arrive when expected? *Must* that new computer work perfectly when you get it home? *Must* other drivers be courteous? The reality is that even in the best circumstances you'll experience a lot of disappointment. People will act in ways you don't like or don't expect. It's unwise to insist that other people and situations always conform to your terms. In fact, it's more likely that you will live a more peaceful and joyful life if you give up trying to control people and situations.

Other-Rating

Other-rating is the strong tendency to overgeneralize about people in a negative way. You condemn another person for a single thing he or she does. As part of this pattern, you use inflammatory language like "dope," "SOB," "idiot," and "moron." You rate the whole person, not just what he or she did or said.

But the problem with this type of thinking is that all of us do a lot of good things and some bad things. Some people do more bad deeds than others, but even those people do some good deeds once in a while. An annoyingly slow driver may be on the way to a volunteer job at a school, or an irritating telemarketer may be trying to earn some extra money for the community ambulance corps.

Every person you know and love will occasionally act in a way that's disappointing to you. When that happens, what is the best way for you to think? Whether you're at work, with your family, at a party, or on a date, when you label someone harshly for doing something you dislike, you interfere with your ability to preserve your relationships and maintain the connections that enrich your life.

Self-Rating

Self-rating is exactly the same irrational thought pattern as other-rating, only with your evaluations directed at yourself instead of at someone else. When things don't go well, you may blame or condemn yourself: "I'm a loser, I can't do anything right, I'll never succeed." This pattern leads to sadness, guilt, and more anger, and it reduces your motivation to fix whatever the problem may be. That's because self-rating takes time away from focusing on the specific problem and coming up with a realistic solution.

Distortion or Misrepresentation

Distortion or misinterpretation involves reaching incorrect conclusions about the motives, intentions, or behavior of friends, family members, co-workers, and others. For example, you may see the actions of other people as intentionally offensive. But when you distort or misinterpret someone else's motivations, you don't consider alternative explanations for that person's behavior.

Vishal, a forty-one-year-old midlevel manager in a large corporation, had a supervisor with an abrupt manner. Vishal took his supervisor's behavior as evidence that she wasn't interested in him and even disliked him. But a closer look revealed that Vishal's supervisor acted this way with everybody. She was under great stress. Her abruptness was related to her own difficulties and had little to do with her ideas about her employees.

Step 3. Think Differently and More Effectively in Anger Situations

There is a rational alternative thought for each of the irrational thoughts associated with the six thinking patterns that underlie anger. These rational thoughts will allow you to evaluate difficult situations in a more flexible, less extreme, more reasonable manner. Refer again to practice exercise 2, and turn your attention to part 2 ("Thoughts"). Which irrational thought pattern (awfulizing; low frustration tolerance; demandingness; other-rating; self-rating; distortion or misinterpretation) comes up most often for you during your anger experiences? If there are several irrational thought patterns that occur frequently, work on them in the corresponding parts of practice exercise 7.

Replacing Awfulizing with Moderate Evaluations

If awfulizing is your most typical irrational thought pattern, you may benefit from learning to label hassles in a more moderate manner. Usually "inconvenient," "unfortunate," "bad," or "difficult" is a better description of any trouble you're facing. The point is not to minimize the seriousness of your struggle or discomfort. No one wants to feel rejected or hurt; no one wants to lose money, a job, or prestige. Rather, these words are offered as more realistic descriptions of your experience. Table 7.1 presents rational alternatives to several awfulizing thoughts. Using the table, complete part 1 of practice exercise 7.

Table 7.1. Awfulizing Thoughts and Rational Alternatives

Awfulizing Thought	Rational Alternative Thought
It's *terrible* that my boss treats me unfairly and doesn't recognize how hard I work for the company.	Although I *don't like* the way my boss treats me, there are far worse work situations to be in.
It's *horrible* that my kids keep fighting with each other.	The constant bickering between the kids is *unpleasant*.
It's *awful* that my boyfriend broke up with me.	The way this relationship ended was really *bad*.

Increasing Your Frustration Tolerance

If low frustration tolerance has emerged as a typical irrational thinking pattern for you, it's important for you to see life's difficulties as manageable instead of continually telling yourself you can't handle them. When a problem comes up, it's all right to say you truly don't like it, that it is unwanted, and that you wish it were not happening.

Most problems and misfortunes in life, whether economic, familial, romantic, legal, or medical, do eventually become manageable even if they do not seem that way at the time you originally face them. In fact, Martha Stewart, Steve Jobs, and many other prominent individuals have faced difficulties ranging from imprisonment and humiliation to professional rejection and disgrace but still managed to survive and even thrive. Telling yourself and others that you can't stand or deal with adversity is clearly unhelpful because it undermines your capacity to cope and develop creative solutions. You'll be better served by describing a struggle as difficult or frustrating than by whining and moaning about how you can't cope with it. Table 7.2 presents rational alternatives to several low-frustration-tolerance thoughts. Using the table, complete part 2 of practice exercise 7.

Table 7.2. Low-Frustration-Tolerance Thoughts and Rational Alternatives

Low-Frustration-Tolerance Thought	Rational Alternative Thought
I *can't stand it* when my wife criticizes me.	I *can* listen calmly to my wife's complaints. I'm a mature person who *is able* to hear other people's perspectives.
I *can't deal* with Bob's obnoxious behavior.	Some people will never learn to be considerate. I *can handle* hearing Bob's comments, and I don't have to take all of them seriously.
I *can't take* my kid's crying anymore.	Babies cry a lot. That's part of being a parent. I don't have to get angry, and I *can stand* hearing it.

Giving Up Demands and Becoming More Flexible

Demandingness is a common thought pattern in most anger experiences. Changes in this area will require you to replace words and phrases like "must," "should," or "has to" with language that's less rigid. For example, it's perfectly acceptable for you to think that you'd like your boss to treat you with respect, but it's very different to think that your boss *must* treat you with respect. It's all right to say you want things to be different, but it's less helpful to *insist* that they be different. Table 7.3 presents rational alternatives to several demanding thoughts. Using the table, complete part 3 of practice exercise 7.

Table 7.3. Demanding Thoughts and Rational Alternatives

Demanding Thought	Rational Alternative Thought
James *should* tell the truth.	It would *be better* for everyone if James were honest about what happened. However, there's no guarantee that he'll be truthful.
The office manager *must* respect my seniority.	I *want* the office manager to respect my seniority.
Debbie *should* show up on time for her appointments.	It would be *more considerate* of Debbie to be on time. But she's one of those people who always seems to be running late.

Replacing Negative Ratings of Others with Acceptance

It's easy to make exaggerated judgments about others when they do things you dislike. Changing this irrational thought pattern requires you to replace negative labels ("jerk," "dope," "ass," and so on) with more precise descriptions of people's specific behavior. It's still all right to view some of other people's behavior as bad, but do refrain from making global judgments about those people. Table 7.4 presents rational alternatives to several other-rating thoughts. Using the table, complete part 4 of practice exercise 7.

Table 7.4. Other-Rating Thoughts and Rational Alternatives

Other-Rating Thought	Rational Alternative Thought
Rick is such a *jerk* because he argued with me in public.	There are a lot of times when Rick is thoughtful and well meaning. However, *one quality* I don't like about him is that he sometimes says nasty things about me in front of others.
The office manager is a *real moron.* What a *fool* (or *jerk*) she is!	Even though the office manager made this unfair decision, she's *treated me well at other times.*
Austen is a little *monster.* He never listens to the rules.	Austen is *still very young* and has a lot to learn. I hope his parents can help him be better behaved.

Accepting Your Own Fallibility

If you typically label or rate yourself harshly when you make a mistake, experience a setback, or act carelessly, then you can make a change by becoming more accepting of your behavior and by differentiating your specific behavior from your total view of yourself. Rating yourself as a totally bad person not only will contribute to your anger but also can lead you to feel guilty and depressed. Table 7.5 presents rational alternatives to several self-rating thoughts. Using the table, complete part 5 of practice exercise 7.

Table 7.5. Self-Rating Thoughts and Rational Alternatives

Self-Rating Thought	Rational Alternative Thought
I can't believe that I messed up the job interview. *I'm such a loser.*	*I wasn't well prepared* for that interview. Next time I'll be ready.
I'm such an *idiot* for forgetting the appointment.	*I forgot the appointment.* Sometimes, I do things like that. I'll see if I can reschedule.
I'm a *horrible* person for treating Adriana that way.	*I made a mistake* when I treated Adriana like that. Next time I'm in this type of situation, I'll handle it better.

Reducing Distortion or Misinterpretation and Interpreting Others' Unwanted Behavior More Accurately

To change this pattern, you'll have to begin by resisting the urge to jump to conclusions about why others' behavior is crummy. Then you will need to consider alternative explanations. Take into account all facts and evidence related to the situation, and come up with a better interpretation. If you don't know the facts, suspend your judgment until you have more information. Table 7.6 presents rational alternatives to several distorted thoughts. Using the table, complete part 6 of practice exercise 7.

Table 7.6. Distorted Thoughts and Rational Alternatives

Distorted Thought	Rational Alternative Thought
Because my supervisor doesn't listen to my ideas and is always in a rush, it's clear that *he doesn't think my work is any good.*	My supervisor seems to always be in a rush and to never listen to anyone. It might be that he's under a lot of pressure, and *it has nothing to do with my performance.*
Eileen canceled our date at the last minute. She said something came up. *It probably means she isn't interested.* Women are such jerks.	I don't really know why Eileen canceled. *Maybe something serious happened.* I'll call her in a couple of days to see if she wants to get together.
Derek keeps interrupting me when I speak. *He doesn't respect me.*	I've noticed that Derek isn't a very good listener. *He seems to interrupt people a lot.*

Step 4. Practice New Thinking in Your Daily Life

Making a real change requires that you practice thinking more rational thoughts in your day-to-day life. Most people are rather slow to change their thinking, and so this change will take some time, but you can accelerate the process if you practice expressing these new and better thoughts out loud. To get started, pick just one of the six irrational thought patterns, and focus on it as you go about your day. Work on changing just that one pattern. When a problem comes up, try the new thought out in the privacy of your mind. Then find a trusted person to whom you can say this thought out loud. For example, you can say to your wife or your husband, "I realize now that I actually can tolerate my boss's behavior. It's silly for me to whine about what a jerk he is. I'm going to learn to take his actions in stride." Then, after you feel confident that the new, rational way of thinking is becoming more automatic for you, try working on another irrational thought pattern. Use your new ways of thinking over the next few weeks. See how this change feels. See if it helps.

Key Points

☑ Your thoughts are products of your personal history and learning, and so your thinking isn't the gospel truth and may not always be accurate, realistic, or helpful.

☑ Pinpoint which of the six irrational thought patterns are common for you during your anger episodes.

☑ Replace your awfulizing thoughts with more moderate evaluations.

☑ Replace statements that reinforce your low frustration tolerance with statements that emphasize your ability to cope with problems.

☑ Give up statements that express rigid demands. Instead, make more accepting and flexible statements about the behavior of others.

☑ Refrain from highly negative ratings of other people. Instead, describe others' specific behavior.

☑ Replace harsh ratings of yourself with statements that reflect self-acceptance and willingness to learn from your mistakes.

☑ Resist the urge to jump to negative and distorted conclusions about the actions of others. Instead, consider alternative explanations.

CHAPTER 8

Strategy Five:
Let It Go!

What we think, or what we know, or what we believe is, in the end, of little consequence. The only consequence is what we do.

—John Ruskin

Events outside yourself are rarely the direct cause of your anger. The situation is more complicated. For one thing, your thoughts about events and your interpretations of them are major causes of your anger (see chapter 7). For another, the words you might hear in a conflict situation are not the same as the reality of the situation. They are just words, perceived from movements of air that enter your ear, and these words have less reality to them than you may think.

As a human being, you have the capacity for what psychologists call *higher cognitive activity,* or the ability to think about situations and judge them. That makes you different from a hyena or an alligator. A wild animal's protective anger is made up mostly of biological urges. Yours is made up of biological urges plus the cognitive activity that allows you to interpret events and make decisions. When you *think* you have been mistreated, neglected, rejected, misunderstood, gossiped about, or cheated on, that thought contributes to your experience of anger.

Like every other human being, your biological and genetic heritage and your evolutionary past have programmed you to make a habit not only of thinking about situations but also of judging them and reacting to them. As a result, you have a strong urge to rush to judgment, and that urge is natural. But you are not limited by biological, genetic, and evolutionary factors. As a human being, you have the remarkable ability to *let go of your thoughts.*

In this chapter, we'll look at thoughts and judgments through the double lens of *acceptance* and *commitment.* These two words are associated with

Acceptance and Commitment Therapy (ACT), developed by the psychologist Steven Hayes. In terms of anger management, the keys to this approach are acceptance of your angry thoughts (that is, just noticing them without acting on them) and commitment to living a life based on your core long-term values. This is different from the strategy of changing the content of your thoughts (see chapter 7).

Acceptance: Noticing but Not Reacting to Angry Thoughts

Your thoughts, actually, are neither true nor false. They're just your thoughts, which means you can stop giving them so much power. To use this technique effectively, the first step is to simply become aware of your angry thoughts, without giving in to them:

- You're driving your ten-year-old son to soccer practice, and he's playing videos very loudly on his phone, even though you've already asked him twice to turn the phone off. You may be thinking, *Are you so stupid that you can't turn the damn thing off?* And you may want to yell, "Stop acting like a jerk!"

- Your boss says, "I've been hearing that you're not pulling your weight on the sales floor. Other employees say you're lazy." Your first reaction may be to think, *That's not true! I am going to find out who's saying that and figure out how to get even.*

In both of these situations, it would be easy for you to allow your thoughts, which are almost automatic, to drive angry actions, especially in the second case, where continued rumination and vengeful behavior would be likely. But another option would simply be to recognize that such thoughts are not reality and then move beyond them.

In this approach, as you tune in to your immediate thoughts in any situation, you may find that they're helpful thoughts, or unhelpful thoughts, or thoughts that are not even related to your current circumstances. Whatever your thoughts may be, the key is to accept them *as thoughts*, mental constructs that may or may not reflect reality. You do not have to react to your thoughts, and your thoughts need not propel you to any type of action, angry or otherwise. Using this approach, you can learn to become an observer of your thinking and to behave in ways that are more aligned with what you believe is most important in life. You can stand outside yourself, so to speak, and observe what is happening in your mind. You don't have to let yourself be bullied by the ideas running through your head. (That's right! Thoughts can be bullies.) Instead, you can practice adopting an open, curious, receptive attitude toward your thoughts and urges, even when those internal experiences are unpleasant. You can just allow your thoughts to come and go, without struggling with them, without trying to change them, and without acting on them.

Consider, for example, the possibility that you do not have to think of yourself as an insensitive person just because someone says, "You never think about me," and that you do not have to think of yourself as stupid just because someone says, "You don't know anything, do you?" Again, like an outsider, you can just observe what you are thinking, without immediately acting on your thoughts. For example, you may be thinking *This guy needs to be taught a lesson* or *I'm not going to take this crap* or *She's a lying bitch—I'll get even with her!* But whatever you're thinking, a thought is still just a thought. It's not reality. So practice listening to yourself, without judging or taking action. Your goal is to unhook your angry thoughts from your actual behavior.

Commitment: Pledging Yourself to Your Values, Your Highest Priorities, and Actions That Support Them

The second step in using the ACT approach to anger management is to become aware of your values. Your values are a reflection of what is important to you in life, of what makes your life worth living. You can also think of your values as large-scale life directions that continuously receive your attention across your entire lifetime.

For example, you may value being a respectful, supportive parent. At times, honoring this value may mean attending your child's soccer games and dance recitals. It may also mean supporting your child's decision to join a math club rather than a football team. As time goes on, it may mean being respectful of your teenager's decision to go to a particular college, or not to go to college at all and join the Peace Corps or the armed services instead. Sometimes honoring your value of being a respectful, supportive parent will be tough, not just for you but also for your child, and of course the circumstances in which you express this value will change as your child matures.

But the underlying value of being a respectful and supportive parent will continue to manifest in a variety of ways. Maybe you'll provide financial or career guidance for your daughter after her college graduation, for example, or maybe you'll babysit your son's children so he can pursue an activity important to him.

If you are like most people, you have never articulated your values, and so you remain relatively unaware of what they are. Figure 8.1 lists several dozen words and phrases that represent core values commonly held by adults. Take a look at that list now. Do any of those words or phrases resonate with you, and with what you feel is most important in life? Then ask yourself these five questions:

1.   What do I value? (Identify your top two or three core values.)

2.   What do I want out of life?

3.   What forces are pulling or pushing me away from my life priorities?

4.   What actions can I take now to move myself closer to my values?

5.   How can I continue to move toward my values in the future?

These five questions will help you consider what you actually value in life and then begin to move beyond your immediate angry thoughts and urges.

But there's one more very important question to ask yourself: "To what extent are my angry thoughts consistent with my life priorities?" In most instances, you will notice that your angry thoughts and urges toward impulsive actions are not aligned with what you consider to be most important in life. Therefore, when you act on such thoughts, you undermine your values and your long-term happiness. By contrast, when you figure out your underlying values, it becomes easier for you to make decisions in line with your priorities, and your choices are guided by factors that will lead you toward a life worth living. In this sense, clarifying your values can act as a powerful motivator for making changes.

For example, it is pretty obvious that if you want to live life as a parent whose priority is to be understanding and wise, then yelling at and demeaning your child is inconsistent with that value. Let's say your fourteen-year-old son has told you that he feels like a girl, and that he has felt this way most of his life. If your core value is to be a supportive, caring, accepting parent, how do you react? Do you say, "It's just a phase—snap out of it"? Do you regard

achievement	fame/recognition	poise
adventure/challenge	friendships	popularity
authenticity/ genuineness	happiness/pleasure	recognition
	honesty	reputation
authority	humor	respect
autonomy/ independence	influence	security
	inner harmony	self-respect
balance	justice	service
beauty	kindness	spirituality/religion
community	knowledge	stability
compassion	leadership	status
competence	learning	success
contribution	love	trustworthiness
creativity	loyalty	understanding
curiosity	openness	wealth
fairness	optimism	wisdom
faith/inner harmony	peace	

Figure 8.1. Common Core Values

what your child has said as crazy, and do you worry about what others will think? Or do you take a moment and focus on your values? In that case, you might say to your child, "Wow! It must be difficult for you to talk to me about this. Tell me more about what it has been like for you. I want to be helpful, and I want you to be happy." Hearing this kind of information from a child sets off all kinds of thoughts and alarm bells in a parent. Transgender, gay, bisexual, and lesbian adolescents face many difficulties in society, and they're statistically much more likely than other teens to think about and attempt suicide. It can be a challenge, but you'll be a much more helpful parent if you can hear this information from your child, not react to your angry urges or angry thoughts, and then act according to your values of love, openness, and kindness.

All of this leads to the idea of *committed action*. You have the ability to think about your thoughts, your impulses and actions, and your values. The goal is to commit yourself to a life in which your values and actions are congruent with the everyday decisions you make. That may not be easy, and you'll need awareness as well as a lot of practice in order to bring yourself to the point where you are deliberately choosing actions that are consistent with your values, not with your angry thoughts. But you can certainly develop that awareness and put in the practice. The decision is yours.

An example may help. Imagine that the job of managing your anger and living by your values is like driving a school bus. The driver's job is to attend to traffic lights, the flow of other cars, and so forth, so that the kids arrive safely at school. They may be singing, yelling, and shouting out all kinds of nonsense—just like your unruly thoughts. And just as the driver is aware of the commotion but pays no attention to most of it, you do not have to pay attention to or act on the thoughts running through your head. Your thoughts are like background noise. They're like the kids on the bus. No one would expect or want the driver to stop the school bus or run it into a ditch just because some kid called her a name, but that kind of angry behavior is exactly how people often react to their own thoughts—as if their thoughts are not just true but also require an immediate reaction.

Sticks and stones can break your bones, but names can never hurt you unless you let them. It's true that words do matter in some situations. But it's also easy to forget that *words are just words*. When others call you nasty names or criticize you or make you the target of their anger, you have two choices:

1. You can choose to hear these words (and to see your own thoughts) as perfect representations of reality, taking them to heart and immediately mounting a strong reaction.

2. You can simply hear the words and let your thoughts flow easily through your mind, recognizing that words and thoughts are not reality.

To improve and enrich your life, choose to take only those actions that are consistent with your core values. The key is to slow yourself down, move away from autopilot reactions, and decide whether what you feel like doing is aligned with what you value most in life. If so, you are on the path toward handling adversity, improving your relationships, and increasing your happiness.

Key Points

☑ Your thoughts are not reality.

☑ You can learn to calmly observe your thoughts, accept them, and refrain from reacting strongly or impulsively.

☑ Values represent large-scale life directions that require continuous attention across a lifetime.

☑ It's important to review your values and clarify which ones are most important to you.

☑ If you're honest with yourself, you can acknowledge that your angry thoughts are usually not consistent with the larger priorities of your life. With that insight, you can discern the extent to which your angry thoughts are helping or hindering your efforts to live by your highest values.

☑ When you commit yourself to actions that are consistent with your values and your highest priorities in life, those actions will improve and enrich your life over time.

☑ It is possible for you, right now, to start noticing your angry thoughts and feelings without acting on them or giving in to them.

CHAPTER 9

Strategy Six:
Forgive

The stupid neither forgive nor forget; the naive forgive and forget; the wise forgive but do not forget.

—Thomas Szasz

If you look carefully, most people's lives are filled with all kinds of problems, disappointments, and conflicts. As noted in earlier chapters, most such events don't meet a real definition of "awful" or "terrible."

Nevertheless, your anger may be due to one or more quite serious events. You, a friend, or a family member may have been injured or even maimed in a beating or a sexual assault. You or a loved one may have been the victim of religious, sexual, or racial oppression or even of a terrorist attack. Events like these can lead to anger that lasts a lifetime, anger that often comes with an intense desire for justice and revenge. You may feel bitter. You may think over and over about the harmful event. And you may be unable to move forward with your life. If you or your loved ones have suffered any of these kinds of incidents, we offer our sympathies and wishes for better times in the future. At the same time, if your personal anger has developed from problems with your children, your spouse or partner, or a friend, you may be able to improve your relationships with many of the SMART "choose and use" strategies in this book.

In spite of reasonable efforts, however, it's sometimes impossible to work toward solving the problem that led to your anger. If you've had something of great value stolen from you in a burglary when you weren't at home, the offender probably isn't even known to you. Or the person who harmed you, and with whom you're angry, may be unwilling or unable to meet with you to work things out. He or she may have moved far away, may be in prison, may have developed a mental illness, may have died, or may be otherwise unavailable to talk with you about what happened.

Fred had a happy marriage, two children, and a good job, but he was still bitterly angry at a former girlfriend who had unexpectedly rejected him when he was a twenty-one-year-old student. She had no interest in talking with him about what had happened years earlier.

Marie, forty-three years old, was still angry at her father, who had worked long hours when she was young and had basically been an absentee parent as he tried to provide for his family. Now, at eighty-one, he had developed Alzheimer's disease, and there was little point in Marie's talking with him about her disappointment and anger.

Whether the event that triggered your own anger was of major or minor significance, a basic question is "Can the problem be remedied?" If so, move in that direction with the strategies presented in this book. If not, it may be time to forgive and move on with your life. After all, the goal is always to reduce your anger and your ruminations about the triggering event, which are likely, in the long run, to be more harmful to you than to anyone else.

Interventions that involve forgiveness are related to the thinking strategies presented in chapters 7 and 8. Those strategies focus on seeing situations logically and accepting the realities of life. Was your anger triggered in a minor way, as when your child spilled her drink on the kitchen floor? Was your anger trigger moderate, as when your ex-wife once again refused to listen to your ideas about what's best for your children? Or was the trigger major, as in a robbery or an assault? Whatever your anger trigger may have been, thoughtful analysis followed by forgiveness will move you along the path toward a calmer, happier life because forgiveness emphasizes a larger perspective and letting go.

Why Forgiveness Is Important

Forgiveness is important because of what happens if you *don't* forgive. Later in this chapter, we'll outline specific steps you can take to develop forgiving responses to the disappointments, misfortunes, or hurts you experienced in the past. For now, we'll describe some *unforgiving* ways to react to past events, including the responses that follow:

- Ruminating on or replaying a hurtful past event

- Holding a grudge about an old hurt

- Avoiding people or places connected to a hurtful event in the past

- Using alcohol and/or drugs to cope with past hurt

- Fantasizing about, seeking, or actually taking revenge

We understand that it's not easy to adapt to mistreatment by others. But realistic adaptation to past mistreatment, coupled with letting go, is often exactly what's required in order for you to improve your life over the long term, and forgiveness is one way to adapt. An unforgiving response is essentially an unsuccessful strategy for coping with unfairness and misfortune. It keeps you in the role of victim and leaves you powerless because it chains you to the past and to the memory of how someone hurt you. Such a strategy ties up emotional energy and interferes with your ability to create and experience joy and happiness. Because it keeps your anger going, it can lead you into self-defeating behavior and cause you high levels of emotional arousal, which over time can take a physical toll in the form of heart disease or stroke.

Rumination

When you think over and over about a person whose behavior led you to become angry in a particular situation, you may also experience unwanted thoughts and mental images. You may continually replay what the other person said as well as other details about the event, and about how you felt at the time. You may dwell on how unfair the situation was and not be able to stop thinking about how the other person intended to harm you.

Grudges

Nearly everyone has held a grudge at one time or another. Sometimes holding a grudge is a reaction to someone's seriously disappointing behavior.

Perry, thirty years old, and his brother Todd, thirty-six, got into an angry argument when Perry's wife didn't attend a family funeral. Todd described his sister-in-law as "stupid" and "disgusting," and he refused to speak to her and Perry for ten years. Todd's grudge not only altered the relationship between his own family and his brother's family but also had a negative effect on their siblings and parents. Family gatherings and holidays became awkward because everyone had to pick a side.

But people may also hold grudges about very minor things.

Marian, thirty-four years old, wondered aloud why she should take Veronica, her nine-year-old daughter, for ice cream after the child paid no attention to her mother's request that she clean her room. A week had passed since Veronica's infraction, but Marian had forgotten that children often don't remember enough to make the connection between their misbehavior and a consequence that follows a week later. In reality, Marian's taking her daughter for ice cream would have been a bonding experience for them, and Marian's threat not to do so was a disproportionate and untimely response to Veronica's failure to clean her room.

The act of holding a grudge suggests a desire to show power, retaliate, and dole out retribution. But a grudge actually does no good. It's often the product of unrealistic thinking and bad decision making, and its negative effects on the people involved will make improvement difficult.

Avoidance

In chapter 5, we described the kind of short-term sidestepping that can be used as a preemptive strategy for bypassing some provocations. Here, we are talking about a negative, longer-term, maladaptive reaction.

Alex, forty-three, went through a difficult divorce and now avoids social gatherings where his ex-wife's friends might show up. He thinks that some of them may be taking her side, and he tells himself that he doesn't need them. Unfortunately, however, Alex lives in a small town, and his avoidance limits not just his social life but also his growth and his ability to move forward with his life. He has never challenged himself to discover whether seeing his ex-wife's friends at social gatherings would actually be as bad as he imagines.

Alcohol or Drug Use

As mentioned in chapter 4, another form of avoidance is using alcohol or other drugs to deal with anger. Some people use substances to escape from negative thoughts and uncomfortable sensations related to the past. These substances interfere with the ability to put the past in its proper perspective and move forward. Using alcohol and drugs to deal with anger is a high-cost strategy that is likely to lead to a lot of other problems.

Revenge

The most serious and dramatic characteristic of an unforgiving response to misfortune is the desire to seek revenge, or an actual instance of revenge. For some people, revenge is limited to fantasies. We've met many people who have spent a lot of time and energy thinking about how to get back at acquaintances, family members, co-workers, strangers, and others who they think have harmed them. Perhaps that's you. Do you think about how you might tell someone off or let someone have it if you were given the opportunity to do so safely? Maybe you think of ways to create difficulties for someone else, or maybe you consider ways to make another person suffer. Some people write multiple drafts of letters or emails expressing their anger, hoping to come up with words that will hurt their target. But even this type of rehearsal wastes time and energy. And when a direct confrontation occurs, or a letter is actually sent, it rarely causes the offending person to suffer as desired. This is because someone who has led us to become angry has his or her own view of the situation, a view that makes personal sense for that individual.

For other people, angry and vengeful thoughts play out more indirectly, in ways that don't involve or even touch on actual confrontation. Common examples of this approach include gossiping, refusing to cooperate, cooperating only minimally, secretly damaging property, and sabotaging a business deal. For instance, because you're angry about an argument you had with your wife last month, you may decide that you're not going to cooperate with her request that you attend her mother's birthday party, and even if you do attend, you may remain distant and unfriendly.

But even mere fantasies of revenge can set the stage for more serious aggression, as when a gang member follows through on his fantasy and retaliates against a rival gang to even the score, or a high school student who feels misunderstood shoots his classmates, or an employee who has lost her job returns to her former workplace and murders her ex-boss. Revenge takes a serious toll on human life and leads to a great deal of misery and suffering.

Forgiveness and Religion

Traditionally, religious teachings have formed the basis of how people think about forgiveness. Forgiving is central not only to Christianity, Judaism, and Islam but also to Buddhism, Taoism, and other communities of spirituality. If you find it helpful to read religious texts, such as the Bible, the Talmud, and the Koran, then continue along that path, by all means. At the same time, if your anger is of long standing, then you've probably found that it isn't easy to forgive.

Sometimes role models can be helpful. If you think that you would benefit from developing a forgiving outlook, then we recommend that you look at the website of the Forgiveness Project.[21] There you will find personal stories of forgiveness from all around the world, stories that are based on religious as well as nonreligious perspectives and that involve drunk driving, gang violence, sexual and other types of assault, racism, and many other topics.

In our experience, however, most people who want to develop the skills of forgiveness require something more than reading religious books, listening to sermons, or hearing stories about others. We see forgiving as requiring thoughtfulness, understanding, and the practice of specific kinds of behavior that *demonstrate* forgiveness. For that reason, we developed a model for a science-based five-step forgiveness process, which you can use to let go of the past and live a happier, anger-free life. We'll describe the model for our forgiveness process in the next section of this chapter. For now, no matter what your faith may be, and whether you are a believer or a nonbeliever, we hope you'll find it useful to briefly review with us what Christianity, Judaism, and Islam have to say about forgiveness.

Forgiveness in Christianity

The Christian position is shown in biblical quotations like "Father, forgive them; for they don't know what they do" (Luke 23:34) and "For if you forgive men their trespasses, your heavenly Father also will forgive you; but if you do not forgive men their trespasses, neither will your Father forgive your trespasses" (Matthew 6:14–15). Christian forgiveness is guided by the idea that seeking revenge for a grievance isn't the right course of action. Instead, the goal is to allow God to take care of the situation in a fair and just manner.

In Christianity, the goal is to forgive even if the offender isn't willing to repent. This idea is shown in Romans 12:19, which states, "Dear friends, never avenge yourselves. Leave that to God. For it is written, 'I'll take vengeance; I'll repay those who deserve it,' says the Lord." In Christianity, the idea is to recognize that offenders require forgiveness, that forgiving the offender is your choice, that God will eventually fix the problem, and that when you're struggling with forgiving it's useful to pray and talk with someone you respect and trust, such as a pastor or friend.

Forgiveness in Judaism

The Jewish perspective is somewhat different. In Judaism, several forms of forgiveness are recognized. According to Rabbi David R. Blumenthal, a professor of Judaic studies at Emory University, "The most basic kind of forgiveness is 'forgoing the other's indebtedness' (*mechilá*). If the offender…is sincere in his or her repentance, the offended person…should forgo the debt of the offender, relinquish his or her claim against the offender. This is not a reconciliation of heart or an embracing of the offender; it is simply reaching the conclusion that the offender no longer owes me anything for whatever it was that he or she did. *Mechilá* is like a pardon granted to a criminal by the modern state. The crime remains; only the debt is forgiven."[22]

By contrast with Christianity, in Judaism the offended person isn't under an obligation to forgive. Rather, the offender is supposed to be sincere and, if possible, to have planned or taken real steps to correct his or her wrongdoing. This type of forgiveness comes with the expectation that the wrongdoer is repentant. For example, an adult woman whose father abused her during her childhood is expected to grant this type of forgiveness only if her father has stopped the abuse, reformed his character, admitted his problems, and asked her for forgiveness. She's morally required to forgive him only if she thinks he's sincere.

A second kind of forgiveness (*selichá*) is considered deeper. It asks the offended party to understand the offender's life and develop a conception of why the offender behaved badly. If this kind of forgiveness is carried out, it leads to empathy for the offender but not necessarily to reconciliation. Forgiveness of this kind proceeds from the idea that the offender, like all the rest of us, is both human and frail. (This perspective is similar to what you'll find in the model for our forgiveness process.)

Yet a third kind of forgiveness in Judaism involves atonement or purification, the absolute and total wiping away of the act instigated by the offender's nasty intentions. For Jews, only God grants this type of forgiveness, since one human being can't totally purify another.

Forgiveness in Islam

The Koran praises forgiveness, which is defined as overlooking the offenses of a person who has done harm by insulting you, committing physical aggression against you, or damaging your property. Again, the role of revenge is considered, but granting forgiveness is seen as desirable even if the power to get even exists. Muslims recognize that refraining from vengeance is difficult, but they consider it a desirable goal that's made easier with the help of Allah.

According to Dr. Muzzamil Siddiqi, former president of the Islamic Society of North America, it's important to believe in the mercy and forgiveness of Allah, but Muslims are also directed to base their personal, human relations on forgiveness: "Forgiving each other, even forgiving one's enemies, is one of the most important Islamic teachings."[23] Not everyone can do this, but the father of Salahuddin Jitmoud, a pizza delivery driver who was murdered, has set a powerful example of this type of forgiveness.[24]

The Forgiveness Process: A Model

Forgiveness isn't immediate. It isn't like flipping a light switch. Rather, it is a process that occurs over time. It involves a slow mental shift that allows you to *understand* the person who offended or hurt you, even in the face of the wrong that was done, and to partially remove yourself from the role of a victim. Forgiving leads to lowered physical arousal, a calmer body, and the ability to make better decisions and be more effective in everyday life. It involves minimizing the frequency, intensity, and duration of your anger, resentment, and thoughts of revenge. In that way, forgiving primarily benefits the person doing the forgiving.

Our model of the forgiveness process consists of the following five steps:

1. Uncovering anger

2. Deciding to forgive

3. Defining forgiveness

4. Understanding why others behave badly

5. Giving something of value to the wrongdoer

Step 1. Uncovering Anger

The forgiveness process begins with the recognition that you've suffered a real injustice. You've experienced psychological suffering or rejection or neglect or possibly physical pain, and the effects of this harm have been truly negative. The anger that was triggered may have been minor, moderate, or severe, and the trigger itself may have been serious or trivial.

- Maybe the woman in front of you in the supermarket checkout line took a long time to dig dozens of coupons out of her purse.

- Perhaps a good friend of yours revealed one of your personal secrets.

- Maybe you lost money to an unscrupulous stockbroker or were the victim of some other financial scam.

- Perhaps you lost your job or an opportunity for advancement because you were the target of racism, sexism, or ageism.

- You may have been physically attacked, sexually assaulted, or otherwise greatly injured.

Your anger may have been mild, or it may have been so intense that you could no longer view the world as a good place.

Regardless of why you got angry, the first step of the forgiveness process is to develop full awareness of the specific anger-triggering event and a complete understanding of the anger itself. You may have thoughts and feelings of hate, hostility, and bitterness. And, as noted earlier, you may want some sort of revenge. Nevertheless, you still may not have a full and deep understanding of what happened.

By talking to trusted and supportive friends or family members, or by writing about the experience in a journal, you can increase your understanding of exactly what happened and appreciate the depth of your anger. The important thing is to discuss the event and not avoid your feelings, although it may be best not to act on them. Just acknowledge them. As you bring your anger experience into the open, you'll find that it becomes easier for you to reconstruct and reevaluate what happened. Then you can begin to see a lowering of your angry reaction.

Step 2. Deciding to Forgive

- "Renata actually did spread nasty rumors about me! I *know* it's true!"

- "I can't work with her anymore. I can't stand her. She's crazy!"

When you continue to focus on the triggering event and your inflammatory thoughts about it, all you get is unnecessary additional anger and personal distress. Without forgetting about that event, can you begin to let go of it, as a strategy for improving your life? Consider these basic questions about yourself and your future:

- What might happen to your anger if your thoughts of revenge disappeared?

- If you made a clear, conscious decision to forgive, what benefits might you achieve?

- How much time and effort does it take to keep your anger going?

- Is your anger really helping you?

- Is it possible that with less anger you would sleep better, eat better, have better relationships with your family and friends, do better in school, or advance more quickly at work?

Keep in mind the fact that no one likes being with an angry person. Your anger began as a legitimate response to an injustice, but it won't lead to improved relationships with others. No matter what caused your anger, and no matter how justified your anger is, your anger is likely to become toxic over time. So look at the facts, reevaluate what's going on, and consider making the decision to change, in order to improve your life.

Step 3. Defining Forgiveness

The very notion of forgiveness often seems foreign and unacceptable. After all, why forgive someone who lied to you, stole from you, rejected you, neglected you, or hurt you? But if you're having difficulty with the idea of forgiveness, maybe it's because you don't understand what forgiveness means. If so, you have lots of company, as we've discovered.

We see forgiveness as a process that allows you to untangle the relationship among your *thoughts*, your *actions*, and your *bodily responses*. Forgiving means letting go of your anger. It means being able to think about what happened to you without feeling your heart pound, sweating, taking a drink or a drug, and having thoughts of revenge. Once you've forgiven someone you were angry with, whatever triggered your anger becomes just one more part of your complex, nuanced life, not your life's central or defining event. Whatever triggered your anger may always be a central memory for you, but it no longer defines who you are.

To make sense of what forgiveness is, let's start by considering what forgiveness is *not*:

- To forgive is *not* to *forget* what happened to you.

- To forgive is *not* to *accept* another's mistreatment.

- To forgive is *not* to *excuse* someone else's wrongdoing.

- To forgive is *not* to *be neutral* toward the event that triggered your anger.

- To forgive is *not* to *justify* another's bad behavior.

- To forgive is *not* to *calm down* about a past harm.

And, just as forgiveness is compatible with greater self-awareness and greater understanding of others, there are certain things with which forgiveness is *not* compatible:

- Forgiveness is *not* compatible with *seeking justice and compensation*.

- Forgiveness is *not* compatible with *condemnation*.

Forgiving Versus Forgetting

Forgiving is most commonly confused with forgetting.

More than twenty years ago, when Saria was growing up in India, her cousin raped her. She's never forgotten what her cousin did, but forgiveness has allowed her to change her focus. Now, instead of obsessively recalling the event and thinking exclusively about how much she wants her cousin to be punished, Saria also has childhood memories of good times she shared with her extended family. Although her memories of the rape persist to this day, they are less frequent now, and her cousin's assault against her is only one event in a much larger picture of her childhood. When Saria does think about what happened, and when she talks about it to others, she's relatively calm. She no longer sees her cousin, and she still remembers what he did to her, but Saria truly hopes that he has grown up to be a happy man, one who has changed his impulsive, aggressive behavior and has learned to respect women.

Forgiving Versus Accepting

A good teacher may know that some students have cheated on an examination. But forgiving those students doesn't mean accepting that cheating is inevitable. The teacher doesn't just angrily stew about it. Instead, the teacher works to change conditions in the classroom so as to maximize honest and moral behavior and minimize the probability that the students who cheated will cheat again. In the same way, forgiving a child who has set a fire or assaulted other children doesn't mean being indifferent. It means, in addition to forgiving the child, helping him or her learn to act properly.

Forgiveness doesn't mean passive acceptance, nor does it imply lack of motivation to change what is bad in the world. If you were wrongly hurt, it isn't proper for you simply to accept what happened to you. Forgiveness allows you not only to free yourself from your anger but also to work toward changing your relationships with family members, friends, and others.

Forgiving Versus Excusing

Clara, a forty-one-year-old mother of two, said, "My husband drinks and yells obscenities at the kids. I think drinking runs in his family. His father did the same thing, and his brother drinks every weekend. There are worse things in the world. At least he works and provides money for the family. It's not that bad."

Well, we think it *is* bad! Children are most likely to thrive if they are brought up in a loving, supportive home. It would be better if Clara's husband didn't drink excessively, and if he didn't yell profanities at his children. We would like Clara to forgive her husband, for the sake of her own happiness.

But we also want Clara and her husband to seek realistic solutions for the problematic drinking and yelling. Clara can forgive her husband *and* stop making excuses for him.

Forgiving Versus Being Neutral

Darin is thirty-two years old. When he was a young child, his stepfather sexually abused him. As Darin grew to adulthood, he slowly began to let go of his anger. He forgave his stepfather and was even able to tolerate the man's presence at family functions. But when he and his brothers, sisters, and cousins began to have children of their own, Darin became concerned that his stepfather might sexually abuse those children, too. To protect them, Darin decided to quietly share his painful experiences with his family members who had young children.

Some situations—discrimination and other injustice in the workplace, a teenager's aggression, the oppressive behavior of a dictator, or, as we've just seen, the sexual abuse of a child—require clear action. If you're angry because of the actions of a bully, a tyrant, a terrorist, or some other evildoer, we don't expect you to be neutral. We expect you to take a side and do what you can to prevent the same actions that hurt and angered you from hurting others in the future.

Forgiving Versus Justifying

Francine, forty-two, was married to Cole, a manager in a hardware store. Cole worked long hours, often leaving for work at eight in the morning and not getting home until nine at night. Francine had just given birth to their second child, and the couple was having a hard time making ends meet. As a result, Cole decided to bring in extra cash by working Sundays as a handyman. But his new sideline meant that he now had to promote his weekend business and give estimates in addition to doing the jobs, and before long he was working seven days a week. Without rest, he became argumentative, demanding, and frankly abusive. Francine justified his behavior. "It's the hard work and fatigue that make him do it," she said. "He really loves me. These days I'm not seeing the real Cole."

We did want Francine to understand what was happening, and to forgive Cole. But forgiving him didn't mean sitting back and justifying what he was doing. There's no justification for being downright nasty.

Forgiving Versus Calming Down

Have you ever told an agitated person to just calm down? How did that work? A state of calm, like any other emotional state, doesn't appear on command. Nor is being calm synonymous with forgiving. Forgiveness is a process—much like becoming angry, which requires a genuine trigger. If you want to calm down about something, it won't be as simple as having someone say to you, "Relax! I know what happened was bad, but just let it go."

As Henry discovered, forgiveness can involve becoming aware not only that conflicts exist in life but also that we have a legal process that can resolve some disputes.

Henry hired a moving company for his journey from New Haven, Connecticut, to central New Jersey. He and the company agreed on a price of $4,000 for all the work. The company seemed reputable, and its advertisements promised insurance for any damages that might occur. The move was timely and seemed to go smoothly.

Unfortunately, after he paid the bill, Henry discovered that his $3,000 large-screen TV was damaged. He filed a claim with the moving company and expected a reasonable response. But the company said the damage had probably occurred before the move, and a customer service representative accused Henry of trying to cheat the company.

Henry was furious. He had a number of shouting matches with the company's reps. He wasn't sleeping well, and he was having headaches.

For Henry, forgiving finally meant reducing his anger and thinking more rationally about a better way to handle the situation. He hired a lawyer to sue the company for $3,000. When he told his story to the lawyer, he did so in a calm, subdued way. Henry's calmness wasn't a sign that the financial loss had come to mean less to him. Rather, it showed that he had put the loss in perspective and was leaving the matter up to the legal process.

You don't just have to chill out about someone's bad behavior. Forgiveness can mean reducing your agitation, changing your thinking, and allowing a dispute to come to a fair resolution through other channels and means.

Forgiving Versus Seeking Justice and Compensation

Wally, fifty-seven years old, had a son who was murdered by an unemployed drug addict seeking money to buy heroin. The police quickly found and arrested the suspect. At the trial, the district attorney told Wally, "I know that you're hurting and that what happened was a tragedy. You'll see that you'll feel much better once we get this thug behind bars." As expected, the suspect was tried, found guilty, and sentenced to a long prison term. But Wally felt no better. His son was still gone.

We've heard this kind of story many times. The pursuit of justice and other kinds of compensation suggests that an angry victim can feel good only by taking some sort of revenge. But justice and compensation, even financial compensation, do not really make things much better.

Consider all the people who have died after years of smoking cigarettes, or handling asbestos without proper protection. Many of their families sued tobacco companies, or negligent construction companies, after their loved ones developed cancer or mesothelioma and died. But financial settlements, sometimes for large amounts, didn't bring their loved ones back. When it was all over, they still grieved.

By pointing out that financial compensation doesn't restore such profound losses, we're certainly not taking the side of negligent construction companies, or of tobacco companies that lied to the public for many years. What we're saying is that true forgiveness doesn't demand compensation. It's an act of understanding—and sometimes mercy—that, hopefully, leads to less anger and less distress for the person originally harmed.

It's also important to remember that justice and financial compensation may temporarily produce good feelings, but those feelings may wax and wane. Forgiving means something much more than feeling good and being compensated. And in many situations, as when a person has been cheated of life savings, or forced to become a child soldier, or wrongly incarcerated, there's no adequate compensation for the wrong that was done.

Something more personal than a criminal conviction or a financial set-tlement is necessary if you want to move forward with your life. But letting go of your anger, bitterness, and fantasies of revenge doesn't mean giving up your desire to make your life better. The perpetrator you're angry with is still accountable for the offense. Justice may or may not be served, but *you* have to be in charge of your anger. No matter what happens, you'll be better off and healthier if you have less personal bitterness. We're with Gandhi: "If we practice an eye for an eye and a tooth for a tooth, soon the whole world will be blind and toothless."

Forgiving Versus Condemning

Condemnation reflects a feeling of moral superiority. But in our years of life and professional practice, we've learned that we all live in glass houses.

The biblical verse "Let he who is without sin, cast the first stone" (John 8:7) ends the well-known story of the woman who was found to have commit-ted adultery and was brought to Jesus Christ by scribes (that is, lawyers), as a test of whether Jesus was overly liberal. Jesus didn't condone her behavior, but he also didn't condemn her as a person. Instead, he thought the scribes were hypocrites. He forgave her and told her not to commit adultery again.

Blame and condemnation have no place in true forgiveness. Ask yourself whether you've ever made a mistake. We have! We both recognize that we've tried to live good lives and help others, but we also know that we've some-times acted in ways we later regretted. We hope that others haven't con-demned us for our human mistakes. We try to give others the benefit of the doubt when we observe bad behavior, and we hope you'll consider doing that, too.

Step 4. Understanding Why Others Behave Badly

It may seem odd, but in this step you come to understand and have com-passion for the person who offended or hurt you. For example, to move in this direction, it may be helpful to understand the childhood of the offender and what led to the development of his or her hurtful behavior. To do this, you will have to make a mental shift and develop new ways of thinking.

How can you learn to put the triggering event in context? You can try to understand the pressure the person was under at the time of the harmful action. Until recently, for example, it was acceptable in some parts of rural

India to kill female children, and less than two hundred years ago slavery was a normal part of life in the southern United States. Thankfully, these cultural practices have ended and now seem quite extreme. But you still have the challenge of trying to understand those cultural practices that, in combination with human nature itself, may have contributed to the offender's bad behavior. Consider, too, the possible influence of these factors:

- Abuse in childhood

- Drug and/or alcohol use

- Brain dysfunction and/or psychiatric illness, including hallucinations and delusions

- Rules learned for the treatment of women, children, elderly people, criminals, and animals

Understanding the offender doesn't mean releasing him or her from responsibility for the harm that was done. The central goal of this step is to see the perpetrator as a whole person who acted unjustly, in part because of the forces of nature, history, and his or her environment.

Step 5. Giving Something of Value to the Wrongdoer

Perhaps there is a family member you haven't seen in years because of some offensive behavior that led you to feel angry. Secretly, you may still hope the person will suffer for having done you wrong. Or perhaps you're angry at a co-worker who cheated or made accusations against you and then was promoted. You may still be harboring anger when you think of that person.

It may surprise you to learn that forgiving sometimes involves generosity or a good deed that's offered to the person who harmed you. You may even provide attention or time that contributes to the improvement of that person's life. If the individual who triggered your anger is your child or a family member, that probably makes sense, and it's something you would expect to do. But if the person is a stranger, this kind of generosity may be hard to understand, if not altogether unthinkable.

But consider making a gift to that person. When you give that person something, you stop being a victim and start being in control yourself. You take power, since you decide what kind of gift to give, when to give it, and what to say. The gift doesn't have to be a physical object, and it doesn't have to be sentimental. In fact, the gift can be symbolic or a simple gesture of goodwill.

Perhaps you can send a holiday card to a lover who rejected you, expressing good wishes for the future. Maybe you can send the person who wronged you an email, sharing a link to an article he or she may like. Or if the person who offended you is now terminally ill, you can send flowers or chocolates to the hospital or the hospice setting.

If the person who angered you has grown much older, you may see him or her in a debilitated state, and you may then take a different view of the person. If the person has died, you might consider making a gift to a charity or a cause that the person liked or supported. You get to decide what the gift will be, but some sort of action is required on your part. And, surprisingly, as noted earlier, it's *you* who will be best served by this kind of forgiveness and giving. It's *you* who will feel better once you've made peace.

Putting Forgiveness into Practice

Although your anger may seem justified, at some point you have to ask yourself, "What kind of person am I, and what is my anger doing to me?" Reading this book may be a sign that you're already asking yourself that question. Do you want to remain a bitter, angry victim? Do you want to continue spending your time thinking about how you were hurt and how you can get even? Or are you ready to consider taking a step forward?

It's important to remember that forgiveness isn't immediate. It's a process that takes time—possibly a long time. It unfolds differently for each person, and it depends to some degree on the characteristics of the situation and those of the people involved. The time it takes to forgive will be different for everybody and every event.

We've met a number of remarkable individuals who have chosen the path of forgiveness in response to serious unfairness and tragedy. We've met other individuals who decided to hold on to their bitterness and anger. In one dramatic case, a parent who struggled to follow the steps of forgiveness came to form a relationship with his son's murderer.[25] Our conclusion is that people who choose forgiveness move forward more positively with their lives than those who remain unforgiving and bitter.

Other Ways to Move Toward Forgiveness

Some victims of severe oppression write books. For example, Primo Levi wrote about his internment at Auschwitz in order to move toward what he called "interior liberation" and improve his mental health.[26]

Others move past anger by way of scholarship. The neurologist and psychiatrist Viktor Frankl, imprisoned in Nazi concentration camps from 1942 to 1945, developed logotherapy, a specialized form of psychotherapy based on recovering from adverse life events by strengthening trust in the meaningfulness of life and the dignity of people.[27] Frankl himself was no doubt helped by his own contributions to psychotherapy, and logotherapy continues to form part of the curriculum for psychologists, social workers, and counselors in training.

Some victims of past harm who are seeking additional ways of moving toward forgiveness tend to write poetry or stories, create films, meet with other survivors, or simply chat via email to further their personal release from anger and vengeance. Some set up websites to devote attention to and explore their own unique situations. Others find it helpful to keep a simple journal in which they write about each phase of the process of forgiving, a practice that allows them to establish the meaning of harmful events and deepen their forgiveness.

If you think it would be helpful to keep a journal, we recommend that you ask yourself the following questions:

- What exactly am I angry about?

- Who is the target of my anger?

- How long have I been angry?

- What are some of the reasons to keep being angry and to seek revenge?

- How does my anger benefit me?

- What are some of the reasons to let go of my anger and still hold the offending person accountable?

- How does my anger hurt me?

- What was life like for the offender while growing up?

- How might the offender have tried to deal with a bad life situation?

- What prevented the offender from doing so?

- Can the offender in some ways also be seen as a victim?

- How can I develop a forgiving, not forgetting, attitude?

- What can I do to move forward with the rest of my life?

If you decide to keep a journal, think about how private you want your thoughts and writings to be. Everyone approaches this question differently. Perhaps you'll consider your journal to be secret. It may represent an opportunity to talk to yourself and express thoughts you wouldn't want to share with others. Or you may decide to share your thoughts with a close friend or family member. You may find it helpful to talk with someone about what you've written. You may even find that it's better to share your writing with someone you respect but who isn't close to you—a teacher, a member of the clergy, or a psychologist. Each of these choices is acceptable.

When you begin to embrace forgiveness, it's often useful to start small. In fact, it's possible to practice forgiveness in lots of everyday situations. Once you've accepted the idea of forgiveness, you'll find plenty of opportunities to practice it. For example, you can practice forgiveness when someone cuts you off in traffic, cuts in front of you in line, misunderstands your intentions, or criticizes your work. The next time you're faced with this kind of irritating behavior, try these simple steps:

- Recognize that you're having the same old angry thoughts ("He's a real jerk" or "She's so rude" or "I'll show him—I shouldn't be treated like that," and so forth). Try to catch yourself in the act of having those thoughts, and put them on hold.

- Briefly try to guess what may be happening or what may have happened in the other person's life that is causing him or her to behave in a way that angers you.

- Silently, in your mind, wish the other person well.

- Let go of your anger and move on with your day.

After you've gained some familiarity with this approach, you may decide to apply these steps to a more significant event from your past. Over time, responding with forgiveness will become easier, and you'll become more able to decide if a more forgiving attitude makes sense to you.

The Challenge of Forgiving

You may agree that many people who have committed offenses can be forgiven. Maybe you recall a time when one of your children, your spouse or partner, one of your parents, your next-door neighbor, or a good friend of yours behaved badly, perhaps by revealing a secret, telling a lie, stealing, or being unfaithful. With time, however, you may have been able to let go of your anger and forgive the person who offended you.

The challenge as you move forward in life is to develop the skills to forgive *all* the people who have angered you, no matter what they may have done. Throughout history, there have been aggressors who caused the deaths of millions of people, and others who committed savage acts against individuals. Is it possible to forgive a serious perpetrator of evil—a violent person who has committed brutal acts? You may not think so, and of course it's more difficult to forgive a wrongdoer when you or someone you love has personally suffered because of the wrongdoer's actions. But is it wise for people who have been victims of such perpetrators to remain angry, bitter, and vengeful? As the months and years pass, what are the likely effects of continued anger on the well-being of the people who were victims? What would you say about the wisdom of continuing to harbor anger if you were the friend of someone who had suffered from the actions of a terrorist, or who had lost a loved one to a mass murderer or a serial killer?

Actions to eliminate future acts of aggression and reigns of terror are surely warranted. It's important that we heed the words of many Holocaust survivors: "Never again." But can the perpetrators of evil eventually be forgiven by their victims? What is in the victims' best interests? What is the alternative to forgiving?

Forgiveness means changing your mental, emotional, and behavioral reactions. When you forgive, you *think* in different ways about the life of the person who offended and angered you. You think about the forces that led that person to behave badly. Over time, you begin to *feel* less anger when the problem comes into your consciousness, and you may even *act* to help the person who offended you in some way. We hope that you'll consider forgiveness as a way of reducing your anger. For now, we leave you with the words of Archbishop Desmond Tutu of South Africa, who was awarded the Nobel Peace Prize in 1984: "Without forgiveness, there is no future." We hope that your future will be bright.

Forgiving Josef Mengele

Eva Mozes Kor, a Jewish woman, was born in Transylvania, Romania, in 1934. In 1944, during World War II, the Nazis transported Eva and her family to the Auschwitz-Birkenau extermination camp, where the so-called Angel of Death—Josef Mengele, a Schutzstaffel (SS) physician— was conducting a series of infamous medical experiments on approximately 1,400 pairs of twins. Because Eva had a twin sister, Miriam, Mengele selected both of them to remain alive for his experiments.

Mengele's usual procedure was to inject one twin with poison, bacteria, or a virus and then watch to see how disease developed and how long it took for death to occur. When that twin died, he would murder the other twin in order to determine, by comparison, the effects of the disease he had caused. Eva and Miriam were in Auschwitz for nine months, but they survived and were liberated in 1945 at the age of ten.[28]

After the war they went to Israel, where Eva married an American survivor of the Holocaust. Eva then moved to the United States and became a successful real estate agent in Indiana. Miriam, who remained in Israel, developed a serious kidney illness from one of Mengele's injections. Eva donated one of her own kidneys to her sister, but Miriam died.

In 1984, Eva began to develop educational programs for the public, and she founded the organization Children of Auschwitz Nazi Deadly Lab Experiments Survivors (CANDLES). In her personal quest for inner peace, Eva also began a campaign to help surviving victims of the Holocaust learn to forgive. Once an embittered survivor, she had become an advocate for healing.

Eva's path to forgiveness began with a trip to Germany to meet with a German physician, Hans Münch, who had worked with Mengele in Auschwitz. Münch was tried after the war but was found not guilty because he hadn't actually carried out Mengele's experiments. Eva, feeling both anger and anxiety, confronted Münch about the past. As they talked, Münch admitted that he had been present during gassings of Jewish prisoners. "And that's my problem," he told Eva, because he was suffering from depression and nightmares about his time working in the concentration camp. After their meeting, Eva sent Münch a letter indicating that she forgave him.

Eva later asked Münch to join her at a January 1995 ceremony to commemorate the fiftieth anniversary of the liberation of Auschwitz. The extermination camp was now a museum. In front of a group of reporters, Eva read a confession of guilt from Münch. She saw Münch's confession as a statement from an eyewitness that could be used to contradict those who continue to deny that the Holocaust happened. At that commemorative ceremony, Eva made a surprising personal statement: "In my own name, I forgive all Nazis." She wasn't forgetting, justifying, condoning, or passively accepting what the Nazis, and Mengele, had done to her or to the thousands of others who had suffered in Auschwitz. Rather, this was her way of letting go of her personal hurt and emotional pain and moving on.

Eva's statement shocked some survivors. They were deeply angry, and they believed it was wrong to forgive those who had caused their suffering. But Eva saw what she had done as a personal action, and she believed she had done the right thing. "I felt as though an incredibly heavy weight of suffering had been lifted," she said. "I never thought I could be so strong."

Eva found that because she was able to forgive the Nazis, she was also able to free herself from her status as a victim. She clarified the difference between forgiving and forgetting: "What the victims do does not change what happened." Believing that all victims have the independent right to heal in their own way, she said, "The best thing about the remedy of forgiveness is that there are no side effects. And everybody can afford it."

In 2006, Eva Mozes Kor's story was made into a documentary titled Forgiving Dr. Mengele. First Run Features distributes the film, and it's available on DVD. We recommend it for readers who are interested in the forgiveness process.

In April 2015, Eva traveled to Germany to testify at the trial of Oskar Gröning, a former Nazi. During the trial, Kor and Gröning shared an embrace and a kiss, and Eva thanked Gröning for his willingness, at the age of ninety-three, to testify about what had happened more than seventy years before.

Key Points

☑ At first the concept of forgiveness may seem strange and unacceptable. Forgiving someone who has harmed or wronged you may seem impossible.

☑ Remaining unforgiving is associated with obsessive thoughts about the past, grudges, avoidance, and a desire for revenge.

☑ Traditionally, principles of forgiveness have been based on religious philosophy.

☑ The advantages of forgiveness include less physical agitation, less anger, better decision making, a greater ability to enjoy the present, the capacity to move on, and living a happier life.

☑ The five-step model of forgiveness consists of (1) uncovering anger and hurt, (2) making the decision to forgive, (3) defining what forgiveness is and is not, (4) developing an understanding of why another person acted badly, and (5) giving something, no matter how small, to someone who has wronged you.

☑ Forgiveness takes time and unfolds differently for each person.

PART 4

Changing Internal
Anger Experiences

CHAPTER 10

Strategy Seven:
Calm Your Angry Urges with Relaxation, Mindfulness, and Meditation

It is not the mountain we conquer, but ourselves.

—Sir Edmund Hillary

* "Just relax!" "Cool down!" "Chill!" The words are so simple to say. But achieving a real state of relaxation is much more difficult. In this chapter, we will help you understand some basic issues about relaxation and teach you ways to easily achieve it.

Relaxing can help you overcome your normal and automatic tendency to become angry and aggressive when you feel threatened. Notice the words "normal and automatic." In the 1900s, the physiologist Walter Bradford Cannon taught us about the *fight-or-flight response* (now called the *fight, flight, or freeze response*). When animals of all sorts feel threatened, they become aggressive and fight, withdraw and take flight, or freeze in place and hope not to be seen.

Let's look at some examples. A cheetah on the savannah of Africa has killed a gazelle to feed her cubs. As the cheetahs are feeding, a group of lions comes along, wanting to take the food. What to do? The anxious and smart

* *Before you begin this chapter, we recommend that you download practice exercise 10 (Progressive Muscle Relaxation Recording) from http://www.newharbinger.com/42266.*

mother cheetah quickly gives up the food and takes *flight* with her cubs, since lions are much more powerful and can easily kill the cheetah and her cubs. By contrast, if lions approach a herd of elephants grazing with their calves, the elephants will show signs of an angry, aggressive *fight* reaction by flapping their ears, moving their heads in a threatening manner, and making grumbling or trumpeting noises. Elephants can do great harm to almost all other creatures, and so other animals steer clear of them. And many gecko lizards, when they sense a threat, will initially *freeze* in place, hoping not to be spotted by potential predators.

In the animal world, staying for the fight, retreating and taking flight, or freezing in place are natural responses that have developed over millions of years. These responses allow animals to avoid harm and get what they need, such as food. Even within a single species, there's a time for fighting and a time for fleeing. For example, rams, stallions, and other male animals often fight with each other for dominance and for rights to the females of the group, but at some point during the fight, one male gives up and takes flight as it becomes obvious that the other is stronger.

Fight or Flight or Something Else?

You are not an animal in the wild. You have a different kind of brain. You can think, evaluate, and judge situations in a more complex way. You don't simply respond with animal instincts. Nevertheless, all human beings are still partially prisoners of that old and automatic fight, flight, or freeze reaction.

Thinking means using your brain to consider options. It means looking at situations, evaluating, and deciding on an appropriate course of action. It means considering some of the SMART "choose and use" strategies for anger reduction that were introduced in earlier chapters, such as sidestepping a difficult situation, using problem-solving skills to develop a new and previously unthought-of solution, and reducing your angry arousal by rethinking the meaning of a situation. But successfully considering alternatives takes time.

In the animal world, quick and automatic fight, flight, or freeze reactions are valuable. Such reactions can save the lives of offspring, preserve food and the lives of family members, and protect territory. Animals have no choice but to react quickly because the aggression they face from other animals is often life-threatening.

In your world, however, there are two additional factors to consider:

1. Most of the threats you face in daily life aren't *life*-threatening. As we've seen, in your human world you most commonly get angry because you experience being insulted, betrayed, misunderstood, criticized, teased, ignored, or treated unfairly by friends and family members. We understand that some threats, such as a robbery or another type of assault, can lead to physical harm, but most of the things you probably get angry about are far less urgent.

2. As a human being, you possess problem-resolution resources that animals can't rely on. You can turn to rules, regulations, and laws. You can bring your disputes to a teacher, a friend, a parent, a mediator, a lawyer, a small-claims court, and so on. For these reasons, you're usually better off not fighting, freezing, or withdrawing. Rather, the best goal is to seek a negotiated solution that's fair and beneficial to you and others.

The Relaxation Response

Finding a fair solution takes time. You have to sit back and relax a bit. You have to take stock of the problem. You have to rise above your natural urge to immediately fight, withdraw, or freeze. You have to decide what to do.

Unfortunately, as we saw in chapter 9, simple words (like "Why can't you just relax?") can't bring about relaxation. But if you can practice relaxation properly, it will slow your reactions down and give you an opportunity to develop a more thoughtful response to anger-triggering situations.

Like the automatic fight response, the *relaxation response* is built into human nature.[29] When this response is triggered, certain brain chemicals are released, and you begin to breathe more slowly and need less oxygen. Your blood pressure drops and your heart rate decreases. You have fewer disruptive thoughts about your problems. The relaxation response can be brought on in many ways, but no matter how you attain it, you become able to think more clearly, act more in keeping with your values and self-interest, react less impulsively to problems, and make more positive choices. Learning relaxation techniques so you can remain calm in the face of provocations is an important way for you to interrupt the anger sequence.

Remember, though, that we're talking about the development of a learned reaction with which you can counter your impulsive urges to act. It takes practice, and you probably won't achieve the deepest state of relaxation until you work at it for a while. Many people can learn relaxation by themselves, but of course some find it easier to work with a skilled professional who can help bring the relaxation response on more quickly. However you accomplish it, learning to relax is an important skill in its own right. Relaxation improves your capacity to deal with many life problems, and it calms your body, with long-term health benefits.

Progressive Muscle Relaxation

In the 1930s, Edmund Jacobson, an American physiologist, developed a technique known as *progressive muscle relaxation* (PMR), a conscious self-control strategy that helps you relax by tensing and releasing various muscle groups. This is not only the most common but also the simplest technique for you to use as you develop your own relaxation response. After some practice, you'll easily be able to tell when your muscles are in a state of tension and when they're relaxed. (You may want to consult a physician if you have muscle-related complaints, orthopedic conditions, or ailments that could be affected by this activity, but if you're able to do the types of physical activities that most adults can do, these procedures won't be difficult for you.)

Eventually you'll be able to bring on the relaxation response while interacting with real-life anger triggers (see chapter 11). But start by practicing PMR in private. Find a block of time (about thirty minutes) when you won't be disturbed. Turn off your cell phone, make the room semidark, and get as comfortable as possible (use the toilet beforehand, if necessary). It's ideal to do PMR while sitting in a comfortable chair, preferably a reclining armchair, although lying on a bed is all right, too. Wear loose clothing and comfortable shoes, or no shoes. Take off your eyeglasses, any heavy jewelry, and your necktie, if you're wearing one. Leave your legs uncrossed.

Begin by closing your eyes and taking a few deep breaths, inhaling through your nose and exhaling through your mouth. The idea is to get a slow rhythm going. Then start alternately tensing and relaxing specific groups of muscles (shoulders, arms, hands, legs, feet, and so on, starting from your head and moving down to your feet, or from your feet to your head, whichever direction you prefer). You don't have to focus too much on tensing. The key is to relax and release each muscle group voluntarily.

You'll get the best results if you complete the entire tense-and-relax sequence once a day until you reach the point of being able to quickly relax any muscle tension you may be feeling. Spontaneous sighing is a good sign! If thoughts come up that interfere with relaxation, just gently bring your focus back to the sensations in your muscles and the rest of your body. If you're very tired, you may even fall asleep. That's not a problem, and it can be pleasant to drift off to sleep while relaxing, but remaining awake will be more helpful to the development of your voluntary relaxation skills.

Practice exercise 10 is a twelve-minute audio recording that you can use as you're learning progressive muscle relaxation. Regular practice will get you to the point where you can do PMR without the recording. But if you find that progressive muscle relaxation is not to your liking, then you have lots of other options, such as mindfulness, meditation, rhythmic and deep breathing, the use of calming words, yoga and other kinds of exercise, massage, prayer, chanting, and experiences in nature, including proximity to and immersion in water.

Mindfulness and Meditation

If you find that progressive muscle relaxation is not for you, there are other options. *Mindfulness* and *meditation* are specific techniques that originated as Buddhist practices but are now part of the secular mainstream. Sometimes they're referred to as *mindfulness meditation*, but they're actually separate skills, although their positive effects can be amplified when the wakeful awareness of mindfulness is combined with formal meditation. Like PMR, these two techniques bring about experiences that many consider similar to relaxation. They involve focusing on the present moment (since you can't be at peace if you're regretting the past or worrying about the future) and learning to simply observe or notice your surroundings without reacting to them.

Mindfulness: Awareness of Your Outer Life

Mindfulness is the practice of present-moment awareness of the world around you. You can use it in any situation while you're awake. In these days of the supposed need for multitasking, mindfulness allows you to focus on and be actively aware of what you're doing while you're doing it.

Take cooking, for example. Cooking can sometimes be a mindless activity. To cook mindfully, you might say to yourself: "I'm cooking. I'm putting oil into the frying pan. Now I'm putting in broccoli and carrots. A carrot fell on the floor. It looks very orange against the white floor. I'm covering the pan. The broccoli looks green. It smells good. I am tasting a small piece of broccoli. It's hot and crunchy. My skin is sweaty. I'm opening the window." Try to focus on all five of your senses. The goal is simply to notice and name or describe your experiences and behavior, without evaluating them. In other words, you make no judgments, such as *good, bad, right, wrong, lazy, weak, strong, kind,* or *mean.* Anger emerges partially from evaluations and judgments—that is, thoughts—and so learning to observe your experiences and behavior without evaluating them can be a powerful eliminator of anger.

What happens if you live without present-moment awareness? You spend your life on autopilot. You don't truly enjoy and appreciate the everyday meaningful moments and experiences. You miss out on the pleasures of friends, family, and food, the joy of a glass of wine or a soothing shower, and the beauty of the sky. You minimize and don't fully receive compliments from others. You miss out on life as you are thinking about the past or the future, neither of which you can do much about. Lacking awareness of the present moment can also prevent you from listening to your body, which may be telling you to sleep more or eat better foods or reduce your stress by making some of the lifestyle changes we discussed in chapter 4.

One way of looking at mindfulness is to consider the goal of developing what Buddhists call *beginner's mind.* Try to see, hear, smell, taste, and feel everything—people, events, words, voices, emotions—with full attention, and as if for the first time. Most of us, for example, after we've been with people for a while, start to anticipate what they will say; we judge their reactions, and we wait for them to finish speaking so we can talk. There is little listening, which is an art to be cultivated. So take a few moments today to have a conversation with your spouse, a friend, your child, or one of your parents, and be fully present, listening carefully to what the other person is saying to you. Don't judge the person or the words. Inhibit your urge to respond. Mindful listening will improve your relationships because open, respectful listening will strengthen your communications and connections with the people who are important to you.

Meditation: Awareness of Your Inner Life

Meditation is a way of reducing arousal and finding peace by reducing your inner self-talk. The typical way to do this is to focus on a sound or mantra, an image, the flame of a candle, or your breath. The idea is to have your thoughts just float by like clouds while you are meditating, and not to see your thoughts as perfect representations of the world. They're *thoughts*, not reality. If you can look at them from afar, so to speak, it will be easier for you to see how your thinking can be problematic, and how focusing on the past and the future can waste time and energy.

By meditating and just being a witness to your thoughts, without being attached to them, you can detach yourself from what Buddhists call *monkey mind*, a figure of speech suggesting that most of our thoughts are like wild monkeys jumping up and down and swinging from branch to branch. Those thoughts lead us from our uncontrollable past to a highly unknowable future and then back again. But if you give your mind something else to focus on, you can achieve a degree of calmness.

We're focused on anger reduction, of course, but meditation has been linked to many other benefits, including improved thinking, increased physical vitality, improved functioning of the immune system, and better sleep. Meditating in the morning and again in the evening, even for five or ten minutes, can help you achieve enough inner peace to counter your angry urges.

Rhythmic Breathing with a Repeated Word

Remove any tight clothing, and turn off your cell phone. With your eyes closed, sit quietly in a comfortable position. Think about your various muscle groups, from your feet up to your face, and voluntarily let them relax. Breathe in through your nose and out through your mouth. Become aware of breathing in a rhythmic fashion. In a way that is similar to meditation, as you breathe out say the word "one" slowly and silently to yourself. Just slowly breathe in and then out and say "one" to yourself. Breathe easily and naturally, repeating the word "one" with every outbreath. Continue to do this for about fifteen minutes. You can open your eyes to check the time, but don't use an alarm, which might startle you. After you've finished, take a few minutes to sit quietly with your eyes closed. Then open your eyes and remain seated for five more minutes. After five minutes, stand up and resume normal activities.

Avoid doing this exercise right after a meal, since digestion may interfere with the development of relaxation. After a period of daily practice, a relaxation response is likely to emerge with little effort on your part.

Calming Words

This practice also overlaps a bit with meditation. Some people find it helpful to choose a calming word, such as "calm" or "mellow," and then say the word aloud (or simply think the word) in rhythm with the strokes or steps of a repetitive exercise like swimming, walking, or running.

Yoga and Exercise

Many people find yoga deeply relaxing, maybe because yoga's focus on body positioning and breathing serves as a distraction from thinking about anger triggers. You can learn basic yoga skills through a formal class or from a DVD. Like other calming techniques, yoga requires consistent practice.

Having some other type of physical exercise routine can also be helpful. Common options include walking, jogging, cycling, swimming, aerobics, weight training, using a treadmill, and attending classes devoted to spinning, BODYPUMP workouts, and Zumba. The key is to find a physical activity you enjoy, one that matches your level of fitness and that you can easily work into your schedule.

Simple Deep Breathing

Simple, slow, diaphragmatic breathing, without tensing of the muscles, is another way to relax. The way you breathe when you're angry tends to be rapid and shallow. You can counteract this tendency by practicing a breathing response that's the opposite—slow and deep.

To breathe from your diaphragm, lie on the floor on your back. Stretch out comfortably. Place a small book on your abdomen. If you're breathing from your diaphragm, the book will gently rise as you inhale and gently fall as you exhale. It may take you a few tries to get used to this movement: breathe *in*, the book rises; breathe *out*, the book falls. Over the course of several days, practice deep breathing for a few minutes each day until this type of breathing begins to come naturally. Once you have it down, see if you can breathe in a way that re-creates this up-and-down movement of your diaphragm when you're standing, when you're sitting, and at other times as you go about your day.

Prayer and Chanting

Any form of repetitive prayer or chanting, if you do it long enough, will create relaxation. Herbert Benson, a professor at Harvard University and coauthor of *The Relaxation Response*, concluded from many of his studies that all forms of repetitive prayer evoke relaxation and reduce bodily arousal. The key is *repetition* of sounds or words. Praying that requires verbal or muscular repetition brings about relaxation because it requires deep, rhythmic breathing. Therefore, a single prayer isn't enough, since it's the repetitive nature of the experience that creates relaxation.

Repetitive prayer and the resulting relaxation response belong to the histories and traditions of many religions and cultures.

- Jews have a form of repetitive prayer called *davening*, which consists of reciting religious text in a soft, droning manner while bowing or rocking back and forth (thus davening involves verbal repetition as well as repetitive muscular action).

- In Eastern Orthodoxy, continuous repetition of the Jesus Prayer ("Lord Jesus Christ, have mercy on me") can produce the relaxation response, especially for people who repeat it up to six thousand times a day, synchronizing the prayer with rhythmic breathing and using a prayer rope to track the number of repetitions.

- In Roman Catholicism, praying the Rosary is a devotion that begins with the Apostles' Creed and continues with five sequences of the Our Father followed by ten repetitions of the Hail Mary and then the Glory Be. When this devotion is repeated nine days in a row, it's called a Novena.

- Some forms of Protestantism and Catholicism promote the use of a what is called a *centering prayer*, which involves sitting comfortably with eyes closed and then choosing and repeating a sacred word, gently returning the attention to that word whenever awareness of external thoughts develops (similar practices exist in Islam, Confucianism, Shintoism, and Taoism).

Experiences in Nature

You may be able to relax just by taking a walk on a sandy beach and listening to the crashing waves, or going near a field or a forested area early in the evening, when all you can hear is the sound of crickets. If spending time in nature is among your most relaxing experiences, try to make it a part of your weekly routine.

Water

You may have noticed the relaxing properties of water. Take a warm bath, walk along a creek and listen to the rushing water, or stand by a waterfall. Hot tubs, spas, and pools can be very helpful, too. Most of us can't stay angry very long after a few minutes in a bubbling, 102-degree hot tub.

Massage

Tension and anger go along with tight muscles. It's no wonder, then, that so many people feel relaxed after a professional massage. If you don't like having a stranger work on your body, an electric massage wand or a massage chair can be a useful alternative.

Videos, DVDs, and Audio Recordings

Bookstores and internet-based vendors carry a wide range of relaxation-related materials. For information and other helpful resources, go to www.youtube.com or www.google.com and type the words "relaxation" or "relaxation techniques" into the search box.

A Menu of Options for Relaxation

When you're faced with a challenge, angry arousal in your body can give you a false sense of optimism and boldness, but that feeling can easily backfire and cause you a lot of pain. In contrast, when your body and mind are relaxed, your responses to life's challenges are more likely to be thoughtful and effective and lead to a calmer and happier life for you.

Traditionally, we've recommended PMR as an effective way to bring about relaxation. And, as mentioned earlier, meditative and mindfulness practices have also entered the mainstream, and many adults and adolescents find these practices beneficial. But connecting with nature, pursuing a religious practice, or participating in other types of alternative relaxation-oriented activities may work better for you.

The techniques described in this chapter are relatively simple to learn and are helpful to most people who practice them. All of them are on the SMART "choose and use" menu of options, and it's your decision whether and when to use a particular technique. Whichever relaxation technique you decide to use, take the time to make it part of your daily routine. When you do, and as you consistently practice evoking a relaxation response that reduces your judgmental thinking and slows down your automatic anger urges, you'll be better prepared to make good decisions about the anger triggers in your life.

Key Points

☑ Like every other animal, you have the *fight, flight, or freeze response* as part of your instinctive reaction to lethal threats.

☑ Most of the difficulties you face are not life-threatening, but the strong physical arousal associated with instinctive reactions will interfere with your ability to respond thoughtfully to problems.

☑ Developing the ability to calm your body and your mind will help you respond less impulsively to challenging situations.

☑ Progressive muscle relaxation (PMR) is a technique you can use to relax.

☑ Mindfulness and meditation increase your awareness of the present moment and allow thoughts to flow through your mind without having to immediately respond to them.

☑ There are many other activities—breathing deeply, exercising, spending time in nature, getting a professional massage, and so on—that can help you experience how it feels to be relaxed and then learn to use your relaxation response as you work on overcoming your normal, automatic tendency to become angry and aggressive when you feel threatened.

CHAPTER 11

Strategy Eight:
Practice Exposure Techniques and Healthier Reactions

In theory there is no difference between theory and practice, while in practice there is.

—Benjamin Brewster

* The secret to learning new skills is practice. Practice is necessary whenever you're learning anything, such as a golf stance, a computer program, or a foreign language. Just reading or thinking about a new skill is not enough. In this chapter, we ask you to face—in your imagination, or in real life—the people, images, words, and situations that ignite your anger. This is what we mean by *exposure techniques*.

Instead of responding to problem situations in your usual tense and angry ways, you'll learn to react with two other responses—relaxation, and more constructive thinking. You're likely to react less to, and be less bothered by, the circumstances that trigger your anger if you practice facing these challenges *thoughtfully*. One way psychologists help people overcome worry, shyness, lack of confidence in dating, and other common problems is by having them face the actual situations that trigger strong emotions. Your anger will lessen when you combine relaxation and constructive thinking with the practice of willingly and consistently facing difficult situations.

* Before you begin this chapter, we recommend that you download practice exercises 11.A (Creating a List of Anger Situations), 11.B (Writing an Anger Scenario), and 11.C (Creating a List of Verbal Barbs) from http://www.newharbinger.com/42266.

When Not to Use Exposure Techniques

Before we show you how to apply exposure techniques to your anger triggers, we want to point out that there are some circumstances in which exposure isn't recommended. We can't list all those circumstances here, but consider these four:

1. *When you lack commitment and motivation.* If you're not committed and motivated to change the way you act when you're angry, then exposure may backfire. For example, instead of working to change your own reactions, you may be secretly focused on trying to change the actions of others, and so you may set yourself up for increased conflict.

2. *When you are actively engaged in substance misuse.* If you're using drugs or regularly drinking alcohol as a way to manage your emotions or avoid problems, then this may not be the right time for you to practice exposure techniques. Your emotions and behavior are usually less predictable when you're intoxicated or high. In addition, substance misuse will interfere with your ability to evaluate your reactions and will make it difficult for you to change. Exposure techniques will be more helpful once your substance use is under control.

3. *When you are depressed or agitated.* If you're prone to serious depression or agitation, then we recommend that you use caution when you attempt exposure techniques. You're the one responsible for monitoring your progress, so you may want to try some of the practice exercises first and see what effects they have on you. If you feel worse, don't proceed. Continue only if the exercises make you feel more confident about handling the challenges you face.

4. *When you are feeling as if you can't control aggressive urges.* If you have a history of assaulting others, and if you believe that by practicing exposure techniques you may harm another person, then please don't proceed. Exposure techniques may still be useful for you, but it would be best if you used them under the supervision of a trained professional.

How Exposure Techniques Work

Exposure techniques can help you do a number of things. Here are some of them:

- Learn new skills in a realistic context

- Habituate to your anger triggers

- Break short-term anger-reinforcement patterns

- Change the way you see yourself and others

Learning New Skills in Real-Life Situations

If you practice relaxation and rational, nonangry thinking without actually facing your anger triggers, you won't be learning these skills in the most beneficial way because you won't be practicing them in a realistic context. It's more useful to practice your new skills in situations that resemble the ones you typically face.

Doug, the Impulsive Father

Doug, thirty-six years old, was a caring father, but he often overreacted, screaming and cursing when his two young sons, Caleb and Jacob, loudly argued with each other. He recognized that his anger outbursts stopped the obnoxious behavior of his children in the moment, but he also saw that his anger had little positive effect over the longer term. In addition, Doug's wife believed that the boys' bickering was perfectly normal and was to be expected.

Doug and his wife attended several counseling sessions, and they eventually agreed that the boys' behavior was reasonably normal and not of major concern, even though it was unpleasant. When Doug examined his thinking about the situation, he identified two thoughts as part of his typical anger sequence: "They shouldn't be fighting" and "I can't stand their bickering."

In counseling, Doug learned that his anger about his son's arguing was magnified by the way he thought about it. He agreed that it would be a good idea for him to replace his demandingness and his low-frustration-tolerance thoughts with two new, rational alternative thoughts: "Bickering is common, so it's silly to demand that our sons stop" and "I can certainly tolerate and accept our sons' bickering without becoming angry."

Doug understood that these two new thoughts were rational alternatives, but when he heard his boys arguing in actual situations, he impulsively reverted to his original thinking patterns. To prepare himself for a better reaction to his sons' arguing, Doug wrote out a description of a typical incident, giving a detailed account of the boys' fighting and of his own reactions. Once he had this scene in writing, he replayed it in his imagination while practicing the new thoughts.

He practiced this exposure technique over the course of a few weeks, and the new way of thinking became more and more natural over time. Before long, Doug was able to use his new thinking to calm his anger when conflict and arguing between his sons emerged.

Habituating to Your Anger Triggers

Human beings have a remarkable capacity to adapt and adjust to unpleasantness of all types. *Habituation* is a term that psychologists use for the process of changing our reactions, over time, to something that initially felt new, threatening, or interesting. For example, let's say you saw a scary movie last night. You felt your heart pounding and your stomach tightening. But what would happen if you saw the same movie twenty-five times in a row? Obviously, the film would lose a lot of its emotional impact on you after you had been exposed to it multiple times.

The same is true for some of your anger triggers. Sometimes you will feel a lessening of your anger if you simply stay in a triggering situation and take the perspective of an observer. Practicing this technique means giving up on changing the other person, making your point, or solving the problem. Of course, this technique is certainly much easier described than performed! But sometimes it really is wise just to observe someone else's unfair behavior without reacting. Yelling at the other person, or thinking obsessively about revenge, may actually distract you from the total impact of whatever is triggering your anger so that you're less able to analyze the situation and develop better responses in the future. Remember, you don't have to react to or act on your angry thoughts (see chapter 8). Over time, you can watch your anger decrease as you learn to become an observer of others' behavior and of your own reactions.

Breaking Anger-Reinforcement Patterns

A lot of people we've worked with say, "Sometimes my anger just comes over me." If this sounds like how you see your own behavior when you're angry, your behavior may be a function of reinforcement (see chapter 1). In other words, your behavior when you're angry may have led to benefits that you haven't noticed. When you've been reinforced (that is, rewarded) for reacting with anger, your anger comes to seem automatic and natural. But you can replace your automatic anger reactions with new kinds of behavior that produce better results if you thoughtfully try out different ways to behave in real-life triggering situations.

Dysfunctional Reinforcement

When Doug yelled at his sons, they immediately stopped arguing. Doug got what he wanted, and so his strong reaction was reinforced. This reinforcement made it likely that Doug would continue his angry yelling. But after a yelling incident, he usually felt out of control, and he recognized that his behavior created distance between him and his sons.

Doug eventually developed a new way of responding to his sons' arguing. Instead of yelling, he took a deep breath and waited five seconds. Then he separated the boys, sending them to different rooms, and he removed their access to computer games for the evening. This new response turned out to be just as effective as yelling when it came to bringing his sons' fighting to an immediate halt. But it was only when Doug looked at the long-term results of his new behavior that he noticed the crucial benefit—a healthier, less volatile relationship with his boys.

Changing How You See Yourself and Others

When you practice exposure to negative circumstances but don't automatically react with anger, something else happens. You learn new things about yourself, other people, and the world around you. And it's not just your view of an offending person that may change when you take time to understand his or her perspective. You may also gain confidence in your own ability to tolerate a difficult situation without an angry reaction.

Less Anger, More Confidence

With practice, Doug began to believe that he was a capable father who could effectively manage the challenges of being a parent. He developed more confidence in his parenting skills along with less intense reactions to the boys' arguments and a better plan for shaping their behavior. Because of his new willingness to face situations differently, he was able to learn and grow.

Working with an Anger Situation

Turn to practice exercise 11.A. Think about a few ongoing situations in which you typically become angry, and in which your reactions generally lead to bad results. You can use the situation you identified in practice exercise 2 as well as others that are more recent. Following the instructions for practice exercise 11.A, list these situations, write a one-sentence description of each one, and for each situation estimate the intensity of the anger you tend to experience. Figure 11.1 shows Doug's responses to practice exercise 11.A.

Now, referring to your list of situations, pick the situation you want to work on first. We recommend that you start with a situation that you've rated somewhere in the middle range, one that you associate with a moderate level of anger (an intensity rating from 4 to 6). The reason for not beginning with your most serious problem is that we would like you to experience some success before you tackle your most difficult situations. For now, put aside the situations with the strongest intensity ratings until you've mastered the following three exposure techniques:

1. Practicing exposure in your imagination

2. Practicing exposure to verbal barbs

3. Practicing exposure in real life

List the situations in which you most commonly become angry. Write a one-sentence description of each situation. Then refer to the intensity scale at the end of this exercise, and rate the intensity of the anger you experience in each situation, with 1 representing almost no anger and 10 representing the strongest anger you've ever felt.

Situation	Rating
My boys are yelling at each other in the next room, and their fighting escalates until I hear a loud crash.	8
Caleb calls Jacob nasty names, and when I tell him to stop, he says, "Jacob started it."	6
I hear my wife telling the boys to stop fighting.	5
At dinner, Caleb and Jacob don't talk to each other.	2
I notice that the boys haven't cleaned their rooms.	2

Intensity of Your Anger	Extent of Your Anger	How You Felt
_____ 1	Almost no anger	Calm, indifferent
_____ 2	Slight anger	Jarred, moved, stirred, ruffled, challenged
_____ 3 _____ 4	Mild anger	Annoyed, bothered, irritated, perturbed, flustered, uneasy, provoked, impelled, cranky, crotchety, distressed, disturbed
_____ 5 _____ 6	Moderate anger	Mad, agitated, pissed off, irked, aggravated, fired up, riled up, all worked up, peeved, indignant
_____ 7 _____ 8	Strong anger	Irate, inflamed, exasperated, fuming, burned up, incensed, infuriated, enraged, hysterical
_____ 9 _____ 10	Extreme anger	Frenzied, vicious, unhinged, up in arms, rabid, crazed, maniacal, wild, violent, demented

Figure 11.1. Doug's Responses to Practice Exercise 11.A

We recommend that you try out all three techniques, even though one or two of them may be a better fit with your anger situation. We also strongly suggest that you practice the techniques in the order in which they're presented here. Then, after you've practiced exposure techniques with a less difficult situation, you can move on to an anger situation that has a higher intensity rating. And as new anger situations emerge in your life, you'll always have the option of facing these new challenges with the exposure techniques described in this chapter.

Practicing Exposure in Your Imagination

Step 1. Create an Anger Scenario

Turn to practice exercise 11.B. Refer to practice exercise 11.A, pick a situation from the middle range of the list you created in that exercise (that is, a situation with an intensity rating of 4 to 6), and follow the instructions for writing an anger scenario. When you write your scenario, begin with a rough draft, and then add even more details to a second version. You may feel some anger as you write your scenario, and that is actually desirable because it indicates that your scenario is on target. Figure 11.2 shows Doug's response to practice exercise 11.B.

Step 2. Practice Relaxation as You Reimagine Your Anger Scenario

After you've completed your anger scenario, find a quiet, comfortable place where you're unlikely to be interrupted. Begin by practicing the PMR sequence you learned in chapter 10. Once you've completed the sequence and feel more relaxed, switch your focus to the anger scenario you created in practice exercise 11.B. Review your scenario: with eyes closed, go through it in your imagination, letting the events in your scenario unfold step by step, as if they were actually taking place. Allow yourself to notice and feel any anger that comes up as the scene unfolds.

Refer to the list you created in practice exercise 11.A, and choose an anger situation with an intensity rating from 4 to 6. Then write out a brief scenario that describes what usually happens in this situation. Include details about the location, the other person(s) involved in the situation, the clothes people are wearing, the weather, the facial expressions of the other person(s), their tone of voice, and so on. Create a vivid scenario that allows you to imagine yourself participating in the situation, not just observing it. If necessary, use extra sheets of paper.

It's early evening, but it's summer, so it's still bright and sunny outside. I'm pulling into my driveway after a long, hectic day at work. There are yellow daffodils in the garden. The front door is blue. There's a crack in the railing. I'm relieved to be home.

As soon as I walk in, I hear Caleb call Jacob a WOAT, which stands for "worst of all time." The boys are sitting in front of the TV and playing a video game. They're both wearing T-shirts, jeans, and sneakers.

Jacob has an irritated look on his face. Neither one of the kids is smiling, and they don't seem to notice me. I'm thinking, They're fighting again. I can't take this bullshit the second I walk in. I feel the muscles in my back getting tight, and my stomach starts to contract.

"Cut it out," I say to Caleb.

"Jacob started it," Caleb says. "You weren't here to see it."

I'm thinking, What the hell is wrong with them? They shouldn't be fighting all the time.

They go on blaming each other, and I try to stay calm. But I feel my face getting hot. My hands are trembling. Just then, Jacob throws the game controller on the floor and stomps off to his room.

Before I can stop myself, I yell at them, loudly enough for both of them to hear, "I've had it with the two of you acting like immature assholes all the time!"

My wife comes into the room and shakes her head. It's clear that she heard me lose it. She looks disappointed.

To avoid an argument with her, I walk out of the room and head upstairs to change my clothes. The stairs are carpeted. The bedroom walls are white, and the bed has a light green blanket on top of it. As I'm changing, I keep dwelling on how irritating it is to have to referee the boys' constant fighting.

I'm upstairs for about twenty minutes. Part of me wants to go back down and have it out with my sons, but I know I'll overreact and start yelling. Another part of me just wants to avoid the whole situation.

I decide to go for a drive. I go downstairs and leave by the kitchen door, slamming it behind me.

Figure 11.2. Doug's Response to Practice Exercise 11.B

Now, with your eyes still closed, use the PMR sequence once again to reduce your tension and arousal. When you're relaxed, go back to your scenario. Review it once more in your imagination, finishing, as before, with progressive muscle relaxation.

As you work with your anger scenario, begin and end each practice session with relaxation. After a number of practice sessions, you'll find that it becomes increasingly difficult for you to feel angry as you reimagine your scenario.

Step 3. Develop a Coping Statement

Once you're able to reimagine your anger scenario without getting angry, you're ready to develop a coping statement, which will replace thoughts that increase your anger with thoughts that help you lessen your anger. To develop an effective coping statement, refer to practice exercise 7, and choose one of the six types of irrational thoughts along with its corresponding rational alternative. Be sure to pick the irrational thought that is most typical for you and most likely to be on target with respect to your anger scenario. If you need to, you can tweak this thought's rational alternative until you come up with a concise coping statement. (For example, Doug created a coping statement from the two rational alternative thoughts he developed in counseling: "Bickering is common, so it's silly to demand that our sons stop" and "I can certainly tolerate and accept our sons' bickering without becoming angry.") Then take a few minutes to commit your new coping statement to memory.

Step 4. Practice Your Coping Statement as You Reimagine Your Anger Scenario

Once again, find a quiet, comfortable location, and reimagine your anger scenario step by step, allowing yourself to notice and feel any anger that emerges. As you begin to feel angry, stop reimagining your scenario, and repeat your coping statement silently to yourself several times. Then return to your scenario and pick up where you left off. As you continue to review your scenario, practice your coping statement whenever you notice that your anger is building. Figure 11.3 shows a portion of Doug's scenario, with his coping statement inserted at points where his anger emerged.

> _As soon as I walk in, I hear Caleb call Jacob a WOAT, which stands for "worst of all time." [The boys' bickering is normal, so it's silly to demand that they stop—I can tolerate it and accept it without becoming angry.] The boys are sitting in front of the TV and playing a video game. They're both wearing T-shirts, jeans, and sneakers._
>
> _   Jacob has an irritated look on his face. Neither one of the kids is smiling, and they don't seem to notice me. I'm thinking, They're fighting again. I can't take this bullshit the second I walk in. I feel the muscles in my back getting tight, and my stomach starts to contract._
>
> _   "Cut it out," I say to Caleb._
>
> _   "Jacob started it," Caleb says. "You weren't here to see it."_
>
> _   I'm thinking, What the hell is wrong with them? They shouldn't be fighting all the time._ [The boys' bickering is normal, so it's silly to demand that they stop—I can tolerate it and accept it without becoming angry.]

Figure 11.3. Portion of Doug's Anger Scenario with His Coping Statement

Step 5. Assess Your Results

Now that you've used relaxation and your coping statement while reimagining your anger scenario, have you noticed that it's more difficult for you to feel much anger? If so, congratulations! You're effectively facing one of your anger triggers.

Practicing Exposure to Verbal Barbs

Before you move on to a more intense anger situation, we'd like you to practice exposure to _verbal barbs_, the anger-triggering things people may say to you as part of a difficult situation. It's useful to practice not reacting to verbal barbs. The steps involved in this type of exposure will help you stay calm when you're the target of someone else's anger.

Step 1. Create a List of Verbal Barbs

Turn to practice exercise 11.C, and follow the instructions for creating a list of verbal barbs connected with your anger scenario. Figure 11.4 shows the list of verbal barbs that Doug created for his scenario.

Refer to the anger scenario you created in practice exercise 11.B. As you reimagine your scenario, recall or imagine three to five negative statements that another person involved in the situation could or did make to you—verbal barbs that could or did trigger your anger. In the left-hand column, write those statements down. In the right-hand column, write an adjective (sarcastic, threatening, angry, dismissive, condescending, and so on) that describes the speaker's tone of voice.

Verbal Barb	Tone of Voice
He started it. You're so unfair!	Accusatory
He deserved it—I'm just getting back at him for what he did to me.	Angry
You are making this situation worse, for our kids and for me!	Condescending
You never listen to my side of the story.	Accusatory

Figure 11.4. Doug's Responses to Practice Exercise 11.C

Step 2. Practice Relaxation in Response to Verbal Barbs

Once you've created your list of verbal barbs, you'll set your anger scenario aside and use progressive muscular relaxation along with your coping statement to respond to these verbal barbs in the same way you responded to your anger scenario. We recommend recording your list of barbs on some type of digital device.

When you record each barb, speak clearly, and for each one try to match the tone of voice you described in practice exercise 11.C. Pause for thirty seconds between barbs, to give yourself time to practice your relaxation skills and use your coping statement. (If you need extra time, you can stop the device and resume playback when you're ready.)

As you begin listening to the first verbal barb, take a deep, relaxing, calming breath. Tense and release one muscle group, and then continue to breathe in an easy, relaxed manner (see "Simple Deep Breathing," in chapter 10). When you hear the second statement, again take a relaxing, calming breath, and then tense and release another muscle group. Repeat this sequence until you've run through your whole list of verbal barbs. Then use the same sequence to go through your list of barbs five more times. It won't take long.

Perform this set of five repetitions several times over the next week, until the verbal barbs no longer produce much anger for you. If you find yourself getting bored as you listen to the recording, then you're becoming successful at hearing verbal barbs without reacting to them.

Step 3. Practice Your Coping Statement as You Listen to Your Verbal Barbs

Listen once again to your recording of verbal barbs, but this time repeat your coping statement during the pauses. As before, run through your list of barbs five times for each practice session. Feel free to stop once your coping statements have become comfortable, automatic responses to the verbal barbs.

Step 4. Assess Your Results

The point of practicing exposure to verbal barbs is to learn to stay calm and use new thoughts in the face of challenging statements. If you're able to listen to your verbal barbs while using relaxation and your coping statement, then you're ready for the third type of exposure.

Practicing Exposure in Real Life

Now that you've had some success practicing relaxation and coping skills in simulations of real life, the next step is to intentionally place yourself in a real-life anger situation. To be successful, it's important that you work hard not to revert to your old, angry reactions. You're practiced now in the skills of staying calm and relaxed, and you're able to understand and rehearse a rational thought in the form of a coping statement, so the challenge is to face an anger-triggering situation and feel minimal anger.

It's important that you not react to anger triggers by making angry statements or using provocative body language or gestures. Your goal is to tolerate a triggering situation, stay calm while hearing negative statements from others, and then exit. Whether you're bringing up a difficult topic with your spouse or partner, interacting with an obnoxious co-worker, or dealing with a rude salesperson, the goal is always the same—to stay calm, leave your angry autopilot response turned off, avoid reacting, cope, and make a graceful exit.

As you take each step, it's important to gauge your success. If you're unsuccessful in a live-practice round, carefully consider what went wrong to get you off track. If you doubt your ability to deal with a difficult situation, then you may need to spend more time practicing exposure in your imagination. If you believe that facing a particular situation in real life is likely to result in a significant problem or a loss (for example, losing your job if you put yourself in a triggering situation with a critical supervisor), then skip live practice for now, or think about getting some professional guidance with this kind of exposure.

Stepping Back, and Stepping Up

Doug's wife was usually the one who responded when she and Doug were together and their sons started to fight. She agreed to step back in order to create more opportunities for Doug to practice his new skills in the situation that was triggering his anger. In turn, Doug agreed to take the lead in dealing with their sons' arguing. It was his job to approach the boys, take a deep breath, think rationally, and solve the problem.

Key Points

☑ When you use an exposure technique, you directly face the people, situations, and words that instigate your anger.

☑ You can use exposure techniques (1) in your imagination, (2) in connection with verbal barbs, and (3) in real-life situations.

☑ Exposure techniques, used properly, give you confidence that you can tolerate difficult people and situations without reacting angrily.

PART 5

Changing Anger Expression

CHAPTER 12

Strategy Nine:
Improve Your Social and Interpersonal Skills

We have talked enough; but we have not listened.

—William H. Whyte

Most anger occurs between people, and so learning to interact more effectively with others will go a long way toward reducing your anger. Successful relationships are also a key to a happier, more peaceful life.

How well you deal with people is largely determined by your social skills. They influence your dating success, your possibilities for marrying or sharing your life with someone, and the type of parent you will become. In addition, your success in your chosen career will ultimately be determined by your ability to connect with others as you negotiate and influence outcomes. Much learning, too, is embedded in a social context, and so, in a general sense, your ability to grow is impacted by how well you communicate with and receive information from other people. In short, your social skills are major determinants of how your life will turn out. But it's surprising how little attention we give to developing our social and interpersonal skills, given how important they are.

The psychoanalyst Karen Horney used to say that all of us, at every moment in time, want to move toward, away from, or against the person we are with. And maybe you've noticed that when you meet someone new—a person you're dating for the first time, your child's teacher, a salesperson, your new dentist, the neighbor who just moved in next door—you have an almost immediate reaction to that person? Within the first few moments, you usually sense one of three reactions:

1. *Hug.* You feel attracted to the person, want to move closer, and desire to continue the interaction.

2. *Ignore.* You feel repelled by the person and want to end the interaction and escape as soon as possible.

3. *Hit.* You feel almost immediate annoyance and anger with the person and have the urge to push, hit, or otherwise move against him or her.

What determines whether you want to hug, ignore, or hit others—and whether others want to hug, ignore, or hit you? Again, social skills have a lot to do with your own and others' reactions.

The good news is that social and interpersonal skills can be learned and improved. In this chapter, we review the underpinnings of more effective relationships. These underpinnings, along with what you say during an interaction, are a subtle mix of things like your body language, how you make and sustain eye contact, your facial expressions, and your body positioning and posture. All these factors contribute to your ability to connect with others. As always, just reading this chapter will not be enough to improve your social and interpersonal skills. If you want to improve how you relate to people, you will have to try out and practice new kinds of behavior in your day-to-day life.

Become Aware of Your Body Language

When it comes to communication, most of us only focus on the words. This makes a certain amount of sense—when we speak with someone, we choose the words that we think will convey our meaning, in all its depth. And yet, as many scholars agree, most of what we signal to others is communicated nonverbally, through our body language; words account for only a small portion of how and what we communicate.

You will get your message across to others more effectively if your body language suggests self-control, confidence, and openness. In contrast, good communication with others will be unlikely if they perceive you as angry and about to pounce. We have worked with many people who were simply unaware that their body language was causing them to come across as angry, aggressive, dismissive, or uninterested. Their words sounded reasonable, but their physical stance, facial expressions, and gestures suggested something different—sometimes different enough to make others uncomfortable and defensive.

Ulysses was a twenty-two-year-old college student. He was smart, hardworking, and energetic. In fact, his enthusiasm and intensity sometimes worked against him because of how he communicated these qualities to others.

Unfortunately, Ulysses frequently turned people off. For example, his questions to his professors came off as critical and challenging, even though Ulysses was attempting to express his curiosity and his desire to learn. Similar problems emerged in his social life. When he talked with fellow students who were discussing everything from movies to politics to other people's social media posts, his comments often sparked arguments. Ulysses also struggled with dating because he had difficulty getting beyond the first get-together.

His main problem was how he came across to others. His poor posture gave the impression that he wasn't listening and didn't care about what others said. When he spoke, his face communicated irritation. He maintained eye contact for too long, and others found this odd. He often interrupted people, and his tone of voice was intense and overpowering. To underscore whatever point he was trying to make in a conversation, he gestured wildly with his hands. During conversations, he also had the habit of standing or sitting just a bit too close to other people.

Ulysses realized that others were not attracted to him. Sadly, though, he never came to understand what he was doing wrong, or the reasons for his constant social rejection.

There are five basic elements of body language:

1. Eye contact

2. Facial expressions

3. Gestures

4. Posture

5. Interpersonal space

Mastering your awareness and use of these five elements will give you a foundation for social effectiveness.

In the end, it will be up to you to practice adjusting your body language in ways that communicate an inviting, open stance. And it's important to note that eye contact, facial expressions, gestures, posture, and interpersonal space do not operate in isolation. They come together in what's known as a *signal cluster*. As such, they can increase or decrease your social effectiveness. Looking at the individual elements of your own body language, and at how you come across to others, is a first step in improving your social skills and becoming a better communicator.

Eye Contact

Effective eye contact with another person feels inviting to that person rather than domineering. Without causing discomfort, it shows your attention to and interest in the other's perspective. In general, too much eye contact can come across as intimidating, threatening, and even insulting. In practice, this means that after five or six seconds, it's important to look away for a bit. Shifting your gaze between the other person's eyes and mouth is a good way to communicate interest in what he or she is saying. The idea is to avoid fixing your gaze solely on one section of the other person's face.

In contrast, too little eye contact suggests lack of interest and lack of attention. We have all had the experience of interacting with people who seemed more interested in texting than in having a real-life conversation. Being distracted by your cell phone, glancing at your computer screen, looking around the room at other people—these are all subtle (and sometimes not so subtle) signs of disrespect.

If you are talking to a small group of people, it's important not to focus on one person for too long. That kind of exclusive, prolonged focus leads others in the group to feel left out of the conversation and increases their sense of disconnection. To hold the attention of the entire group, it's necessary to intentionally shift your attention and make eye contact with everyone.

To learn more about eye contact, go to your local mall and walk into a store. When a salesperson approaches you, talk to that person, but look off into the distance and make almost no eye contact. Notice the effect on the conversation, and try unobtrusively to see how the salesperson is reacting. Then walk into a different store, and repeat the exercise, but this time make excessive eye contact with the salesperson. Again, see how that feels, and observe how the salesperson reacts. In both scenarios, chances are that the salesperson will quickly become uncomfortable and look away. You can also try this exercise with others as you go about your day. With practice, you will increase your awareness of how you're making eye contact and become able to calibrate its use effectively during interactions.

Facial Expressions

Figure 12.1 displays six faces. Two show anger, one shows neutrality, one shows sadness, one shows surprise, and one shows happiness. Can you identify which face expresses which emotion? Pretty easy, right?[30]

Figure 12.1. Facial Expressions: Anger, Surprise, Neutrality, Sadness, and Happiness

Adapted by the authors from Anggi Sukardi's depiction of Steven Gerrard, an English association football player; see https://commons.wikimedia.org/wiki/File:Steven -Gerrard-profile.jpg.

The muscles of your face can communicate interest or lack of interest, happiness or sadness, fear or anger. When you frown with disapproval, purse your lips, pull your eyebrows toward each other, or smirk, you may be putting up a roadblock to good communication. It's possible to put on a poker face and hide your emotions, but most people will be able to read your feelings because you're always revealing them through microexpressions (that is, very small movements of your facial muscles). That's why there is so much to be gained through the practice of facial awareness. The idea is to develop a better sense of your facial communication.

Look again at figure 12.1. Then stand in front of a mirror and try to mimic each expression portrayed in the figure. Notice the muscles of your face and how they feel. Now take another look at the figure and pay particular attention to the face expressing happiness. Practice that expression for ninety seconds each day until it becomes comfortable to the point of being automatic. The idea is for this expression to become a more natural aspect of your everyday appearance. Try not to smirk but to express genuine happiness. You may also notice that you actually feel better because it's hard to feel anger (or sadness or worry) when you are acting happy. This exercise may seem awkward at first, but give it a try.

Gestures

Gestures also play a part in communication. When you keep your hands in your pockets, or on your hips, you may suggest that you're not open to discussion. Pointing at other people or displaying a clenched fist may also suggest a closed attitude. A shoulder shrug, especially when it's combined with a smirk, typically indicates an attitude that says, "I don't know" or "I don't care." Stroking your chin may indicate thoughtfulness—a good sign—but placing your chin in your hand may indicate boredom. And, on a positive note, nodding usually indicates some type of agreement about what is being said.

When you're listening to others, it's good to keep your hands and arms in your lap, or at your side. Crossed arms may communicate annoyance or anger.

When you're speaking, pay attention to where your hands are. Tapping your fingers on a table can indicate that you're annoyed. And when you wave your fingers at someone, you may seem to be demeaning that person. If you tend to gesture a lot, practice keeping your shoulders relaxed and your hands at your sides. It's usually all right to accent a point or two with hand movements, but constantly moving your hands is a distracting mannerism that may come across as domineering. One of us did psychotherapy for years and spent time developing a calm, focused communication style with clients. Learning to stop gesturing so much with the hands and placing them together on the lap improved interactions. It takes a bit of practice to become disciplined in terms of hand gestures, but it's a skill that is quite learnable.

Posture

Whether you're standing or sitting, avoid rounded shoulders as well as a rigid military posture. Your posture gives others information about your attitude and feelings. When you're having a conversation with someone, it's good, as a general rule, to lean forward just a bit at those times when you're listening, to suggest that you're interested in and open to what the other person is saying.

The Wall Stance

To improve your posture, practice the wall stance once a day. Stand with your back against a wall, keeping your heels, lower back, and head lightly pressed against the wall. You should feel straight and aligned. Hold that position until it feels more comfortable (about ninety seconds). Then step away from the wall while maintaining a straight, aligned posture. Try to re-create this posture several times throughout the day.

Height can also affect communication. If you're very tall, be aware that you're usually looking down at others. You may not realize that other people, especially if they're much shorter, may be feeling unequal because of having to look up at you. A pronounced difference in height may leave the shorter person unwilling to reveal personal information to you. When the goal is improved communication, it's a good idea to level the playing field, so to speak, in a way that allows you and a shorter person to look each other in the eye as equals.

Interpersonal Space

When people are communicating, they establish and expect different amounts of distance between themselves and others. It's important to understand the amount of space that is appropriate, since it will vary according to the occasion, the nature of the relationship between the people who are interacting, and cultural norms.

Traditionally, space has been divided into four zones:

1. *Public.* In North America, a formal event like a lecture or a concert is presented in public space, where there is a distance of at least twelve feet between the audience and the speaker or performer. At this distance, there can be little real connection between the speaker or performer and the members of the audience, but the lecture or concert may still be enjoyable.

2. *Social.* When people are between four and twelve feet from each other, they are in social space. This is typically the zone for a small gathering, a university seminar, a work meeting, or an outdoor party. At this distance, most conversation is casual and not threatening. Highly personal information is unlikely to be revealed in social space.

3. *Personal.* When the distance between people is eighteen inches to four feet, they're in personal space. This is typically where interactions take place with good friends or with family members (as when siblings are having a private conversation about a sensitive issue). When personal space is invaded by a stranger, the conversation often stops.

4. *Intimate.* This is the space for whispering, sensual touching, hugging, and kissing. Here, the distance between people is eighteen inches or less. Intimate space is usually reserved for very close friends and romantic partners, and we feel threatened when this space is invaded by others.

Violations of interpersonal space can occur for many reasons, including general unawareness of norms as well as the desire to be domineering or to get too close to someone too quickly. Whatever the reason, moving too close (or keeping too much distance, or entering a zone where you're not expected or don't belong) can be distracting, alarming, and uncomfortable for others.

Become a Better Listener

If you want to be more effective with people, be a good listener first and foremost. People tend to talk more to those who listen well. In addition, when people perceive you as a good listener, they like and trust you more, you become more persuasive, and future interactions with them become more likely.

As a general guideline for conversation, we suggest that you get into the habit of letting others talk more than you do. We recognize that your current interpersonal style may be different from what we are suggesting. We also understand that what we're suggesting may be difficult for you if you disagree with what the other person is saying, or if you think you have something useful to offer. But hold back. Aim to allow the other person to talk 75 percent of the time, reserving only 25 percent of the time for yourself. Give it a try! This one change can make a big difference in how you come across in social situations.

Another social skill related to listening is conveying empathy, or the ability to stand in another person's shoes and see the world from his or her perspective. But simply hearing and understanding others will not be enough. The important part is to *communicate* to other people that you understand their thoughts and feelings.

How do you do that? You practice taking the other person's perspective by using *reflective statements*, or *reflections*. When you use reflections, you listen carefully to what the other person says, and then you restate the person's main point. But this is not mere parroting. Rather, a reflection is a statement (sometimes a guess) about the meaning of what the other person communicated. It is based on *you* statements because its focus is the other person. To begin developing the skill of forming and using reflections, try sentences that begin with "It sounds like..." or "So you're feeling..." or "It seems...." Here are some examples:

- *Sounds like* you're feeling really upset about the argument with your boss.

- *It seems* like you're pretty fed up with this situation.

- *So you're* looking forward to getting away from work for a while.

- *You're feeling* angry that you didn't get the chance to speak with her directly.

- *You* think this whole situation is unfair.

Reflections can feel unnatural at first, and it takes time for most people to get comfortable with using them, so expect a bit of a learning curve. One of the best ways to develop fluency with this skill is to pay attention to the other person's reaction after you use a reflection. If your reflection is on target, the other person will continue talking, will probably nod, and may even express enthusiastic agreement: "Yes—you totally understand!" When a reflection misses the mark, you'll see a facial expression of disagreement, and the other person may correct your statement, possibly providing additional information: "No, I'm not upset that he was late. It's that he lied to me."

Again, don't just parrot what the other person said, word for word. Instead, try to understand the deeper meaning of the communication. For example, if Kevin says, "I'm really pissed off that my ex-wife keeps interfering with my plans to visit the kids," you wouldn't want to just say, "So you're pissed off that your ex-wife keeps interfering with your plans to visit the kids." But you *could* say, "Sounds like you really want to see your kids" or "So your ex is getting in the way of you seeing your kids" or "You're feeling pretty angry when you think about her behavior." Try to grab the essence of what the other person is telling you. If you do, you'll see the other person nod, continue to talk about the topic, and possibly state his or her agreement with you. When you use a reflection, you show that you truly understand the other person's viewpoint, regardless of whether you fully agree with it.

The skill of reflecting is also useful when you're the target of someone else's anger. Perhaps your partner has accused you of being uncaring, or your teenage son has complained that you don't trust him. Using a reflection is a good way to show that you're listening, and it's one of the best ways to defuse someone's anger at you. Remember, the goal is usually to arrive at a mutual understanding and find a solution that works for both of you. Listening is always a critical first step toward this goal.

Overall, there are many benefits to incorporating reflections into your interpersonal style. Reflecting allows you to better understand and clarify what is being communicated. It makes room for the other person to talk, since you're focused more on listening than on trying to make your own points. When you reflect properly, the other person feels understood. Reflecting becomes incredibly valuable once you've reached a level of fluency and can respond constructively to all sorts of statements in different social situations.

Approach Others with Curiosity and Open Questions

Have you ever interacted with someone who asked you a question but wasn't really interested in your answer? It was as if that person was just waiting for his or her own turn to speak. Or have you ever tried to have a conversation with someone who pummeled you with so many questions that the conversation felt more like an interview, if not an interrogation? To avoid making these communication mistakes yourself, try to elicit information from others in a way that allows the interaction between you and the other person to feel like and *be* a genuine conversation. The key is to emphasize *open questions* in your communication style.

You may already know the difference between open and closed questions. In brief, a closed question ("Where did you grow up?") can be answered with minimal information, whereas answering an open question ("What do you remember about your first day of school?") requires more elaboration. But using open questions in a real-life conversation is more challenging than it seems.

When you ask an open question, it's important to deliver it from an exploratory, curious standpoint: "Tell me, what is it that most concerns you about your son?" Other people are actually very interesting when you take the time to understand them. And after you've asked an open question, shift into listening and using reflections. When you combine open questions with reflections, you'll notice improvement in the quality of your conversations. Once a day, make a point of asking an open question with real curiosity, and follow up with reflective listening.

To aid your understanding of open questions, table 12.1 provides several examples of how closed questions can be converted to open questions. As you look at the table, notice how one open question is likely to elicit more information than a barrage of closed questions. An open question produces more of a story.

Table 12.1. Converting Closed Questions to Open Questions

Closed Question	Open Question
Are you married? How many kids do you have? Do you have stepchildren?	How would you describe your family?
Are you working? Are you retired? How many times have you changed jobs?	How has your career changed over the years?
Did your supervisor blame you for the mistake? Have you had it with your job? Are you going to quit?	What are your major concerns about your situation at work and your relationship with your supervisor?

Project an Upbeat, Positive Attitude

To be more effective with people, it's important for you to develop a positive, upbeat attitude. This doesn't mean that you can't ever talk about your problems or struggles. It just means that you should become more aware of what you are broadcasting to others.

A useful way to think about this issue is to look at the ratio of your positive comments to your negative comments in social situations. If you are like many of the people we have worked with, the content of what you say to others on a daily basis has become automatic, perhaps even overly negative.

Pam, a thirty-four-year-old single woman, lived in a large cosmopolitan city and was a successful insurance company executive. She was smart and financially comfortable, but she struggled with dating and with maintaining close friendships.

The problem was that Pam, although attractive to look at, was a downer to be around. First, she was constantly complaining about minor symptoms and discomforts, such as a skin rash, a sore ankle, or simple

fatigue. Most people quickly lost interest in her and withdrew after a few minutes of listening to the tale of her latest medical appointment. Second, most of her spontaneous comments were negative. For example, when she went out to a restaurant with friends, she complained nonstop about the service or the quality of the food. Third, she frequently gossiped about other people, criticizing her recent conversations with them and disparaging their posts on social media. Fourth, in even the most casual conversation, Pam was so quick to disagree that she seemed to be picking a fight.

Several times, Pam had gone on group tours to foreign countries. These adventures had generally started off well, but by the end Pam would find herself disconnected and isolated from her fellow vacationers. Of course, this pattern only served to feed her complaints and criticisms and reinforce her negative style.

Pam never seemed to notice what was going well. She rarely complimented others, reported good news, or appreciated what was positive about her life. And because she was so unwaveringly pessimistic, people rarely sought her out. But Pam was unaware of her automatic patterns, and so she suffered years of anger and loneliness.

This kind of interpersonal negativity has been amusingly portrayed in the "Debbie Downer" sketches on *Saturday Night Live*. But in real life, negativity like this is no laughing matter. If you are not sure where you stand on the issue of automatic negativity, try keeping track of your comments and adding up how many are positive and how many are negative during a morning or an afternoon at work, at home, with friends, or in your romantic relationship. If you skew toward the negative in particular situations or relationships, then it may be time for you to work on projecting a more cheerful, affirming, optimistic persona. There's no single way to inject more positivity into your communication style, but you can make a start by considering the suggestions that follow in the rest of this chapter.

Lead with Warmth, Empathy, and Humor

Resist the temptation to start discussions in ways that come across as too stern, overly fixated on solving a problem, or just plain negative. Get in the habit of jumping into conversations with warmth, empathy, and humor.

Then, if necessary, follow up with something more focused or serious. This is a guideline that applies to verbal as well as electronic communication.

For example, ask your colleague about his or her weekend before you get into the details of the latest budget report. And don't begin a conversation with your spouse by saying, "So our dopey son Jack failed his math test—now we have to figure out some kind of punishment." Instead, try this warmer, more empathetic approach: "Jack must have been so into his new video game that he didn't study for his test. I'm sure I did things like that when I was in middle school. Let's sit down with him and figure out what to do next."

Practice Agreeing with Others

Often, instead of simply agreeing with someone else's statement, people respond by finding objections or pointing out alternatives. And sometimes people express disagreement simply to show their power, flaunt their knowledge, or assert their dominance. But if you can agree, then just agree!

For example, suppose Tyrone says, "That was really a nice restaurant. The food was great." His wife might respond by saying, "Yeah, but the service was slow. Didn't you notice that?" Or she might say instead, "Yes, I agree. Let's go back next week." In other words, making a comment about the service is really not that important; she can simply agree that the food was great, and if she and Tyrone do return, it's likely that they'll get a better waiter, and that the kitchen won't be so overwhelmed, and that the service will be just fine.

Broadcast Good News

As a first step, stop complaining! People rarely gravitate toward others who are negative. So find things that are going well in your life, and in the lives of others, and make a point of bringing those things up in conversations.

For example, you can tell people about one of your recent successes, or about something you did that was fun. Be careful, of course, to avoid the other extreme and come off as a self-centered braggart, although a brief mention of something positive in your life is usually okay. But what's even more important is to ask others about what's going well in *their* lives. Again, curiosity, open questions, and reflective listening can be helpful.

Give Compliments

Some people avoid giving positive feedback. And that's unfortunate because psychological research has shown that a powerful way of strengthening desirable behavior is to provide positive reinforcement for it—that is, to give compliments, praise, and attention for what we judge to be good behavior.

When you offer positive feedback, you strengthen your relationships, encourage others' continued efforts to complete tasks, and help yourself and others become more attuned. With practice, providing positive feedback will also help you become more outgoing, in a *good* way. If you compliment other people and express your appreciation of them, they will be drawn to you.

So get into the habit of complimenting others for actions you value. Become a skillful observer of what people do well, and let them know that you've noticed. Show that you recognize others' skills, competence, strengths, and accomplishments. Here, the keys are to highlight *specific* behavior, be genuine, and avoid statements that may seem superficial or insincere. Practice giving one compliment a day to someone, and then notice what happens! Here are some examples of effective compliments:

- I really liked the way you expressed yourself in the meeting the other day, Dinh. You really captured the difficulties that the sales team is having with this new product.

- Miki, it looks like studying for that math exam really paid off. I watched you review the material over the past few nights. It looks like your study techniques worked. Great job!

- Hey, Denise, thanks for reaching out the other day to say hello. It always makes my day when I hear from you.

- The new program you wrote really looks great, Brad! Two clients have already told me how much they like it.

- John, your sense of humor is really fun.

- Keith, you have a certain wisdom that makes others want to talk with you.

- You wrote a really nice report, Maurice. It was clear and thoughtful. Thanks for putting in so much effort.

Accept Compliments

When people are complimented, they often reject or dismiss the recognition of their efforts. If this is you, practice accepting compliments. For example, if a co-worker says, "That was a great presentation," don't respond with "It was no big deal." Instead, say, "Thank you for recognizing my effort. I worked hard on it." Or if your spouse says, "That was great, the way you helped Jane with her homework," you can say, "Thanks." But it would be better if you said, "Thanks. I've been trying to spend more time with her, and I appreciate that you noticed."

Again, we definitely don't want to turn you into a person with an inflated self-image. Rather, we would like you to recognize that when you're given a compliment, it's useful for you to accept it fully. When you accept compliments and thank others for recognizing your talents or efforts, you'll become more aware of your personal skills, and it's likely that your relationships will improve.

Handle Negative Feedback with Finesse

Of course, not all communication is positive. Some involves discussion of problems, difficulties, and inadequacies. We encourage you to be especially thoughtful when such a complicated scenario arises, and to continue with the goal of being warm, upbeat, and positive. Among the most challenging circumstances are giving and receiving negative feedback.

Giving Negative Feedback

If you have to give someone negative feedback, it's best to deliver it in a private setting, in a supportive way, and in a slow, soothing voice.

Laura, a middle school math teacher, was struggling in her job. Parents were complaining, and Laura's students, by comparison with those in other classes, were doing poorly on standardized exams.

Sofia, Laura's principal, arranged a meeting.

"Listen, Laura," Sofia began, "you seem to be having a hard time. I'm not sure why, but there have been quite a few complaints about you. Maybe you don't know how to prepare an organized lesson plan. Whatever the problem is, we're going to have to take some kind of corrective action very soon because the parents are demanding change."

How do you think Laura felt after hearing this feedback from Sofia? How do you think Laura would have felt if Sofia had delivered her message in a different way?

"Thanks for coming in, Laura. I know you've been working hard to raise your students' achievement level. That's a hard one for all of us. But even though you're trying so hard, your students are not doing very well, and you must be feeling frustrated. I was thinking that some consultation with other teachers might help. What do you think?"

Agreeing When You're Given Negative Feedback

Almost all of us, when we're given negative feedback, tend to deny it or make excuses for ourselves. For example, here is how Laura might have responded to Sofia's feedback:

"My class this year is mainly made up of very poor students who come from challenging households. Their parents don't seem to understand that their children are not paying attention in class. That's the main reason their test scores are so low."

But suppose that Laura, instead of becoming defensive, had responded this way:

"Thanks for pointing this out, Sofia. I know my students are not doing as well as I would like, and they're not at the same level as students in the other classes. I appreciate your suggestion about meeting with other teachers and getting some new ideas. We both want the children to be more successful and learn as much math as possible this year. I'll talk with Elissa—she seems to have a good connection with her students. I'll see if she can give me some pointers. Thanks again."

Denial and excuses rarely lead to self-improvement. It's important to be able to accept criticism gracefully and then thoughtfully consider whether you want to change your behavior.

Stop Controlling

Many people who struggle with anger have a tendency to want to control situations or other people. If this is your pattern, sometimes your goal is to obtain a desired outcome or get others to comply with your demands, and sometimes you just want to do what is truly best for another person. Controlling behavior may be obvious or subtle, but there are three things you can do—or *stop* doing—to interrupt it.

Ditch the Criticism

Being overly critical and judgmental can be a way of making yourself feel better at the expense of someone else. After all, if another person has flaws, then perhaps you look better. But a big drawback of propping yourself up this way is that the positive effects, if any, are fleeting. The real problem is that, over the longer term, you become a drag to be around. How many people enjoy spending time with someone who is always criticizing them?

Cut Back on Debate

When you're arguing with someone, you're probably not enhancing the relationship. Others may and will have opinions—about politics, food, movies, and so on—that are different from yours. So accept this truth, and avoid senseless debate.

There are certainly times when it's appropriate to disagree with others, but there's a way to disagree that leads to improved communication.

- Tricia says to Louis, "I think our daughter looks really great in that dress." Louis says, "The dress is okay, but it makes her look fat." A better response from Louis would be "I respect your opinion, but I disagree. I'm concerned that the dress isn't flattering. What do you think?"

- At the automobile dealership, Stephanie says to Alex, "I love this convertible! It's beautiful!" Alex replies, "You certainly don't understand much about value. It's really overpriced for what it is." Instead, Alex could say, "Maybe you'll be surprised to hear this, but I see it differently. The trunk is really small. And the mileage seems low, so filling the tank would be very expensive. I'm not sure this car really fits our budget. What do you think?"

When you disagree with others, they will probably want to defend their positions. That's a natural tendency, as we've seen. But people can have legitimate disagreements, and it's possible that others will profit from your opinions and ideas. If you can deliver your message respectfully, in a calm and relaxed tone of voice, and invite the other person to share his or her perspective, then you'll both have the best chance for constructive sharing and learning from each other.

Stop Offering the World's Greatest Unwanted Expert Advice

Giving unsolicited advice. Providing unwanted solutions. Lecturing. You mean well. But you're coming across as condescending and demeaning. If this pattern fits you, here's a tip. Slow down and *ask permission* before giving advice or offering a solution:

- "Natalie, I've been thinking about the problem you mentioned the other day, and I thought of something that might help. Can I share it with you?"

- "Bill, I have another friend who had the same thing happen to him. Can I tell you what he did that worked out well?"

- "I've seen this type of thing happen before in our industry. Can I tell you what we did a few years back to handle the issue?"

Keep Your Adversarial Relationships to a Minimum

Adversaries in your career, in your family, and in your romantic affiliations can feed your negativity and drain your emotional energy. Remember, the way your life turns out has a lot to do with the way you manage your social world. Your success depends on the support of other people, but when others are on the sidelines rooting for you to fail, success is not what you get.

As you go through life, then, a good rule is to try to limit the number of your truly adversarial relationships. Or, to put this idea more simply, don't collect enemies. What this means in practice is to sidestep problems, smooth out disagreements, and generally let things go whenever you can. (Refer again to chapter 5 for a detailed discussion of these skills.)

Key Points

☑ Most anger occurs between people. Therefore, learning to be more effective in interactions with others will go a long way toward helping you reduce your anger and live a happier life.

☑ An effective interaction involves your awareness of your body language (including your facial expressions, gestures, and posture) as well as your use of eye contact and interpersonal space.

☑ You can use reflections to become a better listener and show empathy.

☑ Your interactions will improve if you get in the habit of approaching others with curiosity and asking open questions.

☑ Starting a conversation with warmth, empathy, and humor can help you project an upbeat, positive attitude. Other aids to projecting positivity include agreeing with others, broadcasting good news, and giving and accepting compliments.

☑ If you pull back from criticizing, debating, and presenting yourself as an expert, you will stop giving the impression of wanting to control others during a conversation.

☑ In general, it's best to keep adversarial relationships to a minimum.

CHAPTER 13

Strategy Ten:
Express Your Anger in an Assertive, Productive Way

The path to power is not dominance over others but the ability to speak up for oneself. The key distinction is the difference between aggression and assertion.

—Hara Estroff Marano

* Now that you've developed some social and interpersonal skills (see chapter 12), it's time to build on that foundation by moving on to a discussion about being assertive—the final SMART "choose and use" strategy for anger reduction. In this chapter, you'll learn the differences between and among *assertive*, *verbally aggressive*, and *unassertive* responses to a problem. You'll also develop an understanding of how to recognize and assert your rights in a conflict or a disappointing situation, without losing the ability to appreciate the viewpoints and rights of others. By repeatedly practicing the assertiveness skills described in this chapter, you will develop an assertive lifestyle.

No matter how good your relationships are with your family members, friends, and co-workers, sometimes they will behave badly, and you will feel annoyed, angry, and even furious. You'll find this strategy especially useful when you are feeling angry and want to express your anger, but in a way that doesn't ruin your relationships.

* Before you begin this chapter, we recommend that you download practice exercise 13 (Developing an Assertive Response) from http:// www.newharbinger.com/42266.

Is it okay to express your anger when others act in ways that are inconsiderate, annoying, and disrespectful? Perhaps you think anger expression is not just okay but actually required in order for others to know exactly where you stand, and so you let it all out, just the way you feel it. Unfortunately, however, others may not like your strong reactions, and you may suffer the loss of family relationships, friendships, jobs, and so forth. Or perhaps you think it's *not* okay to express your anger, because you don't believe you have the skills to do so in a difficult situation. You just don't know what to say. You may be concerned that if you do express yourself, the discussion will get heated and turn into an argument. As a result, you may not be honest about your feelings because you've had difficulty controlling your angry reactions in the past. You may say nothing and fume silently when people treat you badly. This approach often leads to built-up resentment. Then, when you do finally express yourself, you may do so in a way that is too strong, too aggressive, and thus ineffective. This is a common pattern for people who struggle with anger—they don't know how to express their feelings in a productive manner, or how to ask directly for what they want. If these patterns fit you, it's time to learn how to be more assertive in dealing with others.

In 1970, the psychologists Robert Alberti and Michael Emmons developed assertiveness training.[31] Learning how to act assertively goes hand in hand with keeping your anger in check. In fact, assertiveness training is one of the most powerful techniques for anger control that psychologists have ever developed. Assertiveness skills help you express your emotional reactions appropriately, stand up for yourself during conflicts, and negotiate solutions with others in a fair and reasonable way. These skills also minimize the emotional blocks that keep you from acting in your own best interests.

Goals of Acting Assertively

When you act assertively, you use appropriate words and behavior as you try to reduce conflict and work with others to find mutually acceptable solutions to problems. Notice that we said "try." We believe that assertive communication gives you the best chance of working things out, but it isn't a guarantee.

Judith is a forty-two-year-old married executive with two young children. She generally gets along well with Malaya, her boss. Nevertheless, Judith becomes angry when Malaya schedules her for out-of-town business trips without giving her enough notice for the trips not to interfere with Judith's family obligations. To meet Malaya's expectations, Judith usually cancels her plans with her family. On the outside, Judith appears to be flexible and accommodating. On the inside, she feels angry and resentful and is considering finding a new job.

Miguel, a twenty-eight-year-old newlywed, was simply informed by his wife, Angie, that they would be celebrating New Year's Eve with her mother. Angie frequently commits herself and Miguel to spending time with her family, but without asking Miguel first, though he usually just goes along. But the get-togethers with Angie's family don't go well, because Miguel often loses his temper over some minor thing that Angie says or does during the visit.

If Judith and Miguel were to assertively approach the people who trigger their episodes of anger, they might be able to produce reasonable solutions. For example, if Judith expressed her concerns assertively, Malaya might listen and then change the way she schedules Judith's travel. Likewise, if Miguel talked assertively to Angie about how the two of them could schedule weekend and holiday events in a way that still gives appropriate consideration to what Angie's mother wants, they might be able to work out a mutually agreeable plan.

If assertiveness works for you and reduces conflict and distress in your life, fantastic! But we're realistic, so we understand that assertiveness alone may not always produce the desired result. That's why we typically pair assertiveness skills with one or more of the other SMART "choose and use" strategies for anger control. If you find assertiveness skills alone ineffective, you can bring in another skill to help you reduce your anger as you work toward a solution.

Short-Term Goals

In the short term, the goal of assertive communication is to work with another person to solve a particular problem. But the anger that develops from conflict, rejection, and unfair treatment often stands in the way of clear thinking about potential solutions and interferes with people's ability to work together. In other words, there's usually some emotional baggage that has to be recognized and unpacked before a solution can be found.

Of course, a mutually agreeable solution depends on the situation as well as on how cooperative the other person is. When anger between two people is relatively mild, it's often possible to simply brainstorm a solution. For example, Judith and Malaya could decide that Judith will give Malaya a list of workable travel dates, and that Malaya will consult this list before scheduling Judith for an out-of-town trip. The more reasonable Malaya is as a leader, and the more she respects and values Judith as an employee, the more likely it is that she and Judith will reach an agreement. But if Judith's anger toward Malaya is strong and inappropriately expressed, or if Malaya is harboring anger of her own toward Judith, then the anger between them will have to be resolved before a solution can be reached and accepted.

Long-Term Goals

The long-term goal of assertiveness is the development of an *automatic* way to approach difficult situations, a way that involves not only expressing feelings but also reaching solutions. For example, Miguel, recently married, can expect many more family-related conflicts in the years to come; that's normal in any marriage. Therefore, it will be useful for Miguel to learn how to respond automatically in a way that allows him to give appropriate expression to his annoyance while also communicating his desire to resolve the issue at hand. The more automatic Miguel's assertiveness becomes, the more likely it is that he will live a calm, happy life.

When to Be Assertive

It isn't necessary to be assertive in every situation. Again, not all unpleasant behavior has to be confronted, not all disagreements have to be discussed, and not all problems can be resolved. You have to choose which problems call for an assertive reaction and which ones you can let go. In some situations, other SMART "choose and use" strategies, such as making lifestyle changes (chapter 4), sidestepping provocations (chapter 5), forgiving (chapter 9), and relaxing (chapter 10), may be helpful. But if a problem persists within an ongoing relationship that you value, then it's worth your time and energy to try to improve the situation through assertive communication.

How to Be Assertive

When you express your thoughts and feelings assertively, you communicate directly, honestly, and appropriately. Communicating *directly* means meeting and talking with, or writing to, the person with whom you're having a conflict. By contrast, indirect communication includes gossiping, complaining, or having someone else carry your message. Communicating *honestly* and *appropriately* means expressing your true feelings, beliefs, desires, opinions, and preferences at the right time—without sarcasm, without screaming, without exaggeration, and without going on and on.

How could Judith have responded assertively after Malaya, her boss, scheduled business trips for Judith without consulting her first? How could Miguel have responded when Angie, his wife, informed him that she had planned New Year's Eve for both of them without asking him how he wanted to spend the evening?

Judith: Malaya, I felt confused and a little annoyed when I found out you'd planned a trip for me but didn't check with me first. It was a problem for me. I'd like to talk with you about how we can do the scheduling together for my future trips so they can work out better for both of us.

Miguel: Angie, I felt annoyed when I heard we were going to your mother's on New Year's Eve. I was really surprised you didn't confirm that with me. I'd like us to talk about it and figure out how we can be more on the same page in the future.

Judith's and Miguel's assertive responses both have the same three essential elements, and both convey the same overall message:

1. This is *what I feel*.

2. This is the *behavior I didn't like*.

3. This is *what I would like*.

Notice the use of the word "I." An assertive statement usually begins with "I feel…" because that kind of statement makes communication more human, more personal, and more authentic. It can be a statement in response to something that was done, as in "I felt _____ when you…."

Or it can be a statement in response to something that was said, as in, "I felt _____ when you said...." Do you notice what's missing from those two statements? Two things: blame ("*You made me* so angry") and exaggeration ("You behaved so disrespectfully that *I never want to see you again*").

To sum up, then, there are three steps to creating and delivering an assertive response:

1.   Give the other person a clear message about *how you feel*, but not so forcefully that he or she will be unwilling to talk with you again.

2.   Identify the *specific behavior* you find problematic.

3.   Express *what you would like instead*.

How does this formula look in action? Let's say you have a friend who's in the habit of canceling your get-togethers without much notice. The next time this happens, your response could be "You can never be counted on!" Or instead you could say, "I felt annoyed when you canceled lunch at the last minute." Then you could propose a solution: "In the future, I'd like us to make our lunch plans on weekends only, so work won't interfere. What do you think?" Notice how this response also invites your friend to talk some more with you about the issue.

To become comfortable with the three-step formula for assertiveness, you'll have to repeat it a number of times. The best way to do this is to work with practice exercise 13. Figure 13.1 shows Miguel's responses to the exercise.

"I Feel..." or "I Feel That..."?

As the first step in assertive communication, it's important to say how you're feeling. But watch out! If you begin by saying, "I feel that...," you won't actually be able to express a feeling, as in "I feel annoyed" or "I feel concerned." What you'll probably be expressing instead is some kind of judgment. "*I feel that* you should treat me better" is not the same statement as "*I felt sad when* you didn't call me on my birthday." The first statement implies criticism. The second conveys information about you.

Part 1. State the Problem

Briefly describe a recent instance of an ongoing problem that you think can be resolved with assertiveness skills.

My wife, Angie, told her mother we would spend New Year's Eve at her house, without discussing it with me first. I love my mother-in-law but didn't like being left out of the planning for such a significant holiday.

Part 2. Create an Assertive Response

Use the three-part formula for crafting and delivering an assertive response to the issue that triggered your anger.

1. I felt… (Write a feeling: annoyed, uncomfortable, awkward, concerned, sad…)

   really surprised and annoyed.

2. …when you… (Identify the specific behavior you didn't like.)

   told your mother we would go to her house for New Year's Eve without talking to me first.

3. I would like… (Propose a solution and/or ask the person to talk about the issue with you.)

   to talk with you first about plans like this so we can make decisions together and I can avoid being caught off guard again.

Figure 13.1. Miguel's Responses to Practice Exercise 13

Differentiating Assertive, Verbally Aggressive, and Unassertive Responses

When you respond with verbal aggression, you express your feelings and thoughts, but at someone else's expense. You try to take control of the situation by talking powerfully, dishonestly overplaying your reactions, and neglecting the rights of the other person. The message you convey is that your ideas are absolutely correct, and that the other person is dumb if she or he thinks differently. Here is how Judith and Miguel would sound if they responded to their respective situations with verbal aggression:

Judith: Malaya, you were really inconsiderate when you planned that trip for me. My whole relationship with my daughter has been ruined! I'm not going to put up with that kind of crap in the future.

Miguel: Listen up, Angie. I was enraged when I found out we were going to your mother's on New Year's Eve. It ruins the whole holiday! What the hell is wrong with you? I'm not going, and that's that. You'd better be careful about this kind of stuff.

In both responses, the message is "I'm right and you're wrong," "This is what I want, and I'm not interested in what you want," and "We'd better do things my way!" The words convey self-centeredness, blame, and threat. Verbally aggressive responses aren't very effective, and they can be risky. For example, Judith could put herself at risk of being fired, and Miguel would probably create hostility and distance between himself and his wife. Remember, the goal in conflict is to open up communication, but verbally aggressive messages are likely to shut others down or cause them to get defensively angry at you.

When you respond unassertively, you set aside your own feelings and desires to please others. You hold your anger in, keep quiet, and avoid conflict. Here is how Judith and Miguel would sound if they responded unassertively to their respective situations:

Judith: Before the trip was scheduled, I had planned to go to my daughter's school concert, but it's no big deal. I just bought her some ice cream when I got home. There will be plenty of other concerts.

Miguel: I was hoping to spend New Year's Eve with our friends. But we can go to your mother's. I don't care.

All of us neglect our own desires once in a while to avoid a conflict or please someone else. But being habitually unassertive interferes with your ability to build close, honest relationships and can lead to lower self-esteem, tension, and physical disorders like stomachaches and sleep problems.

Verbal aggression and unassertiveness both lead to failure in the long run. Neither response can create the kind of open communication that characterizes a successful relationship with your spouse, your children, your romantic partner, your friends and acquaintances, and your co-workers.

Balancing Your Own and Someone Else's Rights

Let's say you have an ongoing problem with someone, and you've told that person how you're feeling, what you don't like, and what you would like instead. So far, so good. But what if the other person wants something different? How can you be assertive and still respect someone else's needs or wishes?

Sometimes there are specific rules, policies, or laws that regulate behavior. For example, many condo associations require a homeowner to submit an application for permission to change plantings or the color of the front door, and most workplaces have policies governing the length of the workday, the timing of vacations, behavior between co-workers, and so on. But in most situations in which your anger is triggered, there is no established policy or legal authority. You may believe that you've been treated unfairly, wrongly rejected, neglected, disrespected, or misunderstood. What you have to remember is that the goal of being assertive is not to win and get your way every time, at all costs. The goal is to find a mutually satisfying solution, and this means that you have to give some thought to the balance between what you want and what the other person wants.

Ferdinand, a thirty-one-year-old plumber, worked for a small but growing company that served suburban homeowners. Lately he had formed the impression that his employer, Armando, was taking advantage of him by sending him out on a lot of late-night calls. Ferdinand had gone on fourteen such calls over the past two months, but his colleague Max had gone on only three. Ferdinand was angry about having to spend so many evenings away from his family and friends. He approached his boss assertively.

"Armando," he said, "I'd like to talk to you. I was feeling really annoyed yesterday. You sent me out on that late call and let Max go home early. That was the fifth time this week. I'd like to find a better solution for times when there's an increase in late calls so I don't have to take them all."

Armando's response surprised him.

"This has been a real problem," Armando said. "Max has been having a medical problem, so he gets tired easily, and it seems like he's not able to work very well at night. His doctor doesn't know yet what's going on. It might take a while to sort this out."

His employer's response left Ferdinand with a decision to make. He had to balance his own rights with Max's rights and with what was best for the company. Ferdinand wanted a more even distribution of the late-night work calls, but he decided to help Max and the company by taking the extra workload for another six to eight weeks. His decision didn't produce a solution that was fair to him, strictly speaking, but Ferdinand thought he was doing the right thing.

About two months later, Max's condition worsened, and he took a medical leave. Armando hired two additional plumbers, asked Ferdinand to act as their supervisor, and gave him a raise—all because Ferdinand had demonstrated that he was a good communicator, and that he was flexible and willing to help out by finding a workable solution to an unexpected problem.

The optical illusion shown in figure 13.2 is a good representation of something that can be seen in two different, mutually exclusive ways. John and Peter have two separate takes on the image, and they're both correct. Right now they're arguing about the number of bars in the image—John sees four, and Peter sees three—but what each of them could do instead is practice seeing the image from the other's perspective. That's a useful skill for anyone who wants to avoid conflict by understanding why others say what they say and do what they do.

John: "I see four bars. There are definitely four."

Peter: "What? Are you crazy? Look again! Obviously, there are only three bars."

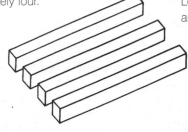

Figure 13.2. Different Perspectives

Why not put that optical illusion to practical use? Think about a conflict you're having with someone. First describe the conflict from your own perspective. You can describe it to a friend, or you can describe it aloud to yourself. (If you're talking to yourself in public, be sure to have a cell phone in your hand!) Then pretend you're the other person involved in this conflict. Describe the problem from the beginning, from the other person's perspective, and be sure to describe as many elements of the conflict as you can from the other person's point of view. If you're not used to thinking this way, it will be difficult for you to consider the problem from any perspective other than your own. But taking the other person's perspective can give you some real insight into the conflict. Try it!

Developing an Assertive Lifestyle

When you're being assertive, be sure you look at the other person, and that you relax. Use not only the social and interpersonal skills you learned in chapter 12 but also the techniques of deep breathing you learned in chapter 10. Maintain a pleasant attitude, and use a firm tone of voice. Be aware of the importance of compromise, and remember that your task is to find win-win solutions. Always listen to the other person—after all, people like to know they've been heard—and be mindful of your body language. Practice and repetition will help you make assertiveness a part of your natural way of reacting. Here are some skills to work into your daily interactions with others.

Practice "Feeling" Statements

Describe what you're feeling (not thinking) or what you felt (not thought) by using statements like these:

- I am feeling annoyed as I hear how you are portraying me.

- Right now I am feeling disrespected, since you are not allowing me to tell my side of the story.

- I can feel myself becoming frustrated, since you seem to just be telling me that I am wrong.

- I felt annoyed when…

- I felt awkward when…

- I felt uncomfortable when…

- I felt happy when…

- I felt irritated when…

- I felt good when…

Get used to making these kinds of statements by giving yourself the assignment to do so twice a day for seven days. Express negative as well as positive feelings, but don't overdo it, or you may come across as self-centered. Notice that when we suggest statements to describe negative events, we often use the word "annoyed" rather than "angry" or "furious." Even though you may actually have a strong or moderately strong feeling, in most situations that involve a social conflict the word "annoyed" will be better received than a stronger word.

Express Your Desires and Preferences

Practice talking in ways that express your opinions or desires. You want your message to be personal and clear, and you want to indicate that you're sharing something of importance. Again, don't express your preferences all the time, but do practice once or twice a day. Here are some examples:

- I liked this movie.

- I enjoy the Museum of Science.

- I'd prefer pizza tonight.

- I'd really like it if we could…

- I'd like to go to _____ on our vacation.

- I hope to see you again.

Describe Behavior and Situations Precisely and Without Exaggeration

When you're talking with others, remember to keep your comments specific and accurate rather than general and excessive. Describe specific behavior instead of making sweeping generalizations. Here are some examples:

- I didn't like the movie because it dragged on too long.

- I really liked the party because Jackie made a point of introducing me to her friends.

- The amusement park wasn't as much fun as I'd hoped it would be, because the lines were too long.

- Jason was really inconsiderate today because he was busy texting while I was trying to talk with him.

Remember, the essential elements of an assertive response are (1) "This is how I feel," (2) "This is the behavior I didn't like," and (3) "This is what I would like instead." Expressing anger in an assertive, productive way is the last of the ten SMART "choose and use" strategies, and we certainly wish you good fortune in your quest for anger reduction. But there are still two more issues for us to address:

1. Let's say you've worked diligently on the ten strategies but are still experiencing problematic anger. That issue is addressed in chapter 14, "What If I Still Get Angry?"

2. How can you combine anger reduction with skills that directly enhance happiness? That issue is addressed in chapter 15, "Live a Happier Life."

Both chapters are found in part 6 of this book, downloadable from http://www.newharbinger.com/42266.

Key Points

☑ Being assertive means (1) expressing your thoughts and feelings directly, honestly, and appropriately; (2) standing up for what you want; and (3) negotiating mutually desirable solutions with others.

☑ It isn't necessary to always be assertive. You'll have to decide which situations deserve your time and energy.

☑ Verbal aggression and accusations make situations worse because they shut others down and increase the likelihood that others will get angry at you.

☑ Being unassertive means giving up your own desires and avoiding problems in order to please others. A consistent pattern of unassertiveness interferes with creating close, honest, healthy relationships.

☑ It is important to consider the other person's perspective.

☑ Being assertive doesn't mean getting your way at all costs. It requires being thoughtful about the balance between what you want and what the other person wants.

Suggested Readings by Chapter Topic

Introduction

Deffenbacher, J. L. "Evidence for Effective Treatment of Anger-Related Disorders." In *Anger-Related Disorders: A Practitioner's Guide to Comparative Treatments*, ed. E. L. Feindler. New York: Springer, 2006.

Kassinove, Howard, and Raymond Chip Tafrate. "Application of a Flexible, Clinically Driven Approach for Anger Reduction in the Case of Mr. P." *Cognitive and Behavioral Practice* 18 (2011), 222–34.

Tafrate, Raymond Chip, and Howard Kassinove. "Anger Management for Adults: A Menu-Driven Cognitive-Behavioral Approach to the Treatment of Anger Disorders." In *Anger-Related Disorders: A Practitioner's Guide to Comparative Treatments*, ed. E. L. Feindler. New York: Springer, 2006.

Chapter 1

DiGiuseppe, Raymond, and Raymond Chip Tafrate. *Understanding Anger Disorders*. New York: Oxford University Press, 2007.

Kassinove, Howard, ed. *Anger Disorders: Definition, Diagnosis, and Treatment*. Washington, DC: Taylor & Francis, 1995.

Mostofsky, E., M. Maclure, G. H. Hofler, J. E. Muller, and M. A. Mittleman. "Relation of Outbursts of Anger and Risk of Acute Myocardial Infarction." *American Journal of Cardiology* 112 (2013), 343–48.

Potegal, M., and R. Novaco. "A Brief History of Anger." In *International Handbook of Anger*, ed. M. Potegal, M. Stemmler, and C. Spielberger. New York: Springer, 2010.

Chapter 2

Averill, J. R. "Studies on Anger and Aggression: Implications for Theories of Emotion." *American Psychologist* 38 (1983), 1145–60.

Chapter 3

Miller, W. R., and S. Rollnick. *Motivational Interviewing: Helping People Change*. 3rd ed. New York: Guilford Press, 2013.

Schumacher, J. A., and M. B. Madson. *Fundamentals of Motivational Interviewing: Tips and Strategies for Addressing Common Clinical Challenges.* New York: Oxford University Press, 2015.

Tafrate, Raymond Chip, and Howard Kassinove. "Angry Patients: Strategies for Beginning Treatment." In *Roadblocks in Cognitive-Behavioral Therapy: Transforming Challenges into Opportunities for Change,* ed. R. L. Leahy. New York: Guilford Press, 2003.

Chapter 4

Coccaro, E. F., D. J. Fridberg, J. R. Fanning, J. E. Grant, A. C. King, and R. Lee. "Substance Use Disorders: Relationship with Intermittent Explosive Disorder and with Aggression, Anger, and Impulsivity." *Journal of Psychiatric Research* 81 (2016), 127–32.

Elliot, A. J., and H. Aarts. "Perception of the Color Red Enhances the Force and Velocity of Motor Output." *Emotion* 11 (2011), 445–49.

Krizan, Z., and A. D. Herlache. "Sleep Disruption and Aggression: Implications for Violence and Its Prevention." *Psychology of Violence* 6 (2016), 542–52.

Kwong, Matthew. "The Impact of Music on Emotion: Comparing Rap and Meditative Yoga Music." *Inquiries Journal/Student Pulse* 8:5 (2016). http://www.inquiriesjournal.com/a?id=1402.

Toohey, M. J., and R. DiGiuseppe. "Defining and Measuring Irritability: Construct Clarification and Differentiation." *Clinical Psychology Review* 53 (2017), 93–108.

Chapter 5

Lohr, J. M., B. O. Olatunji, R. F. Baumeister, and B. J. Bushman. "The Psychology of Anger Venting and Empirically Supported Alternatives That Do No Harm." *Scientific Review of Mental Health Practice* 5 (2007), 53–64.

Seidman, S. A., and J. Zager. "A Study of Coping Behaviours and Teacher Burnout." *Work & Stress* 5 (1991), 205–16.

Chapter 6

D'Zurilla, T., and M. R. Goldfried. "Problem Solving and Behavior Modification." *Journal of Abnormal Psychology* 78 (1971), 107–26.

Nezu, A. M., and C. M. Nezu. "Problem Solving." In *Psychopathology and Health,* ed. J. C. Norcross, G. R. VandenBos, D. K. Freedheim, and N. Pole. Vol. 4 of *APA Handbook of Clinical Psychology.* Washington, DC: American Psychological Association, 2016.

Nezu, A. M., C. M. Nezu, and T. J. D'Zurilla. *Problem Solving Therapy: A Treatment Manual.* New York: Springer, 2013.

Chapter 7

Ellis, Albert, with Raymond Chip Tafrate. *How to Control Your Anger Before It Controls You.* Secaucus, NJ: Carol Publishing, 1998.

Chapter 8

Eifert, G. H., M. McKay, and J. P. Forsyth. *ACT on Life, Not on Anger: The New Acceptance and Commitment Therapy Guide to Problem Anger.* Oakland: New Harbinger, 2006.

Gardner, F., and Z. Moore. *Contextual Anger-Regulation Therapy.* New York: Routledge, 2014.

Kolts, R. *The Compassionate Mind Guide to Managing Your Anger: Using Compassion-Focused Therapy to Calm Your Rage and Heal Your Relationships.* Oakland: New Harbinger, 2012.

Chapter 9

Enright, R. D. *8 keys to forgiveness.* New York: Norton, 2015.

Enright, R. D., and R. P. Fitzgibbons. *Forgiveness Therapy: An Empirical Guide for Resolving Anger and Restoring Hope.* Washington, DC: American Psychological Association, 2015.

Chapter 10

Fried, R. *Breathe Well, Be Well: A Program to Relieve Stress, Anxiety, Asthma, Hypertension, Migraine, and Other Disorders for Better Health.* New York: Wiley, 1999.

Goyal, M., S. Singh, and M. S. Sibinga. "Meditation Programs for Psychological Stress and Well-Being: A Systematic Review and Meta-Analysis." *JAMA Intern Med* 174: 3 (2014), 357–68.

Jacobson, E. (1978). *You Must Relax: Practical Methods for Reducing the Tensions of Modern Living.* 5th ed. New York: McGraw-Hill, 1978.

Kabat-Zinn, Jon. *Wherever You Go, There You Are: Mindfulness Meditation in Everyday Life.* New York: Hyperion, 1994.

Plutchik, Robert. *Emotions and Life: Perspectives from Psychology, Biology, and Evolution.* Washington: DC: American Psychological Association, 2003.

Chapter 11

Deffenbacher, J. L., and M. McKay. *Overcoming Situational and General Anger: A Protocol for the Treatment of Anger Based on Relaxation, Cognitive Restructuring, and Coping Skills Training.* Oakland: New Harbinger, 2000.

Grodnitzky, Gustavo R., and Raymond Chip Tafrate. "Imaginal Exposure for Anger Reduction in Adult Outpatients: A Pilot Study." *Journal of Behavior Therapy and Experimental Psychiatry* 31 (2000), 259–79.

Tafrate, Raymond Chip, and Howard Kassinove. "Anger Control in Men: Barb Exposure with Rational, Irrational, and Irrelevant Self-Statements." *Journal of Cognitive Psychotherapy* 12 (1998), 187–211.

Chapter 12

Ames, D., L. B. Maissen, and J. Brockner. "The Role of Listening in Interpersonal Influence." *Journal of Research in Personality* 46 (2012), 345–49.

Ekman, Paul. *Emotions Revealed: Recognizing Faces and Feelings to Improve Communication and Emotional Life.* New York: Owl Books, 2003.

Kowalski, R. M. "Aversive Interpersonal Behaviors: On Being Annoying, Thoughtless and Mean." In *Behaving Badly: Aversive Behaviors in Interpersonal Relationships*, ed. R. M. Kowalski. Washington, DC: American Psychological Association, 2001.

Moyers, T. B., and W. R. Miller. "Is Low Empathy Toxic?" *Psychology of Addictive Behaviors* 27 (2013), 878–84.

Rosengren, David B. *Building Motivational Interviewing Skills: A Practitioner Workbook.* 2nd ed. New York: Guilford Press, 2018.

Chapter 13

Paterson, R. J. *The Assertiveness Workbook: How to Express Your Ideas an Stand Up for Yourself at Work and in Relationships.* Oakland: New Harbinger, 2000.

APPENDIX A

Recommended Readings for Anger-Related Problems

The following books address problems that may overlap with your anger.

Michael E. Addis and Christopher R. Martell, *Overcoming Depression One Step at a Time: The New Behavioral Activation Approach to Getting Your Life Back* (Oakland: New Harbinger, 2004).

Robert Alberti and Michael Emmons, *Your Perfect Right: Assertiveness and Equality in Your Life and Relationships*, 10th ed. (Oakland: Impact, 2017).

David H. Barlow, Todd J. Farchione, Shannon Sauer-Zavala, Heather Murray Latin, Kristen K. Ellard, Jacqueline R. Bullis, Kate H. Bentley, Hannah T. Boettcher, and Clair Cassiello-Robbins, *Unified Protocol for Transdiagnostic Treatment of Emotional Disorders: Workbook*, 2nd ed. (New York: Oxford University Press, 2017).

Dennis C. Daley and G. Alan Marlatt, *Overcoming Your Alcohol or Drug Problem: Effective Recovery Strategies Workbook*, 2nd ed. (New York: Oxford University Press, 2006).

Jack D. Edinger and Colleen E. Carney, *Overcoming Insomnia: A Cognitive-Behavioral Therapy Approach*, 2nd ed. (New York: Oxford University Press, 2014).

Thomas Horvath, *Sex, Drugs, Gambling, and Chocolate: A Workbook for Overcoming Addictions*, 2nd ed. (Oakland: Impact, 2004).

William Knaus, *End Procrastination Now! Get it Done with a Proven Psychological Approach* (New York: McGraw-Hill, 2010).

Robert L. Leahy, *The Worry Cure: Seven Steps to Stop Worry from Stopping You* (New York: Three Rivers Press, 2005).

Gary D. McKay and Steven A. Maybell, *Calming the Family Storm: Anger Management for Moms, Dads, and all the Kids* (Oakland: Impact, 2004).

William R. Miller and Ricardo F. Muñoz, *Controlling Your Drinking: Tools to Make Moderation Work for You*, 2nd ed. (New York: Guilford Press, 2013).

Seamus Mullen, *Real Food Heals: Eat to Feel Younger and Stronger Every Day* (New York: Avery, 2017).

Barbara Rothbaum, Edna Foa, and Elizabeth Hembree, *Reclaiming Your Life from a Traumatic Experience: A Prolonged Exposure Treatment Program* (New York: Oxford University Press, 2007).

Resources for Finding a Therapist

Research has consistently shown that people who participate in treatment make substantial improvements in anger reduction. Consider contacting one or more of these organizations, which can help you locate a qualified therapist in your area.

Academy of Cognitive Therapy

http://academyofct.org

Click the *Get Connected* link on the *Find a Therapist* button to be taken to the *Find a Certified CBT Therapist* page.

The Albert Ellis Institute

http://albertellisinstitute.org

Click the *Find a Therapist* link at the top of the page to locate a practitioner in your area.

American Psychological Association

http://apa.org

Click the *Psychology Help Center* link at the top of the page to be taken to the *Find a Psychologist* link.

Association for Behavioral and Cognitive Therapies

http://abct.org

Click the *Find Help* link at the top of the page, and then the *Find a CBT Therapist* link.

Motivational Interviewing Network of Trainers (MINT)

http://www.motivationalinterviewing.org

Click the *Trainers/MINT Members* link at the top of the page to be taken to a searchable map showing practitioners' locations.

Universities that have doctoral-level psychology programs are another important source of information for locating practitioners. You can contact a nearby university's psychology department to see if the department has a training clinic, or the department may be able to refer you to a qualified therapist in your area. And, of course, you can get in touch with the authors in our university settings. For our contact information, please visit the publisher's website: https://www.newharbinger.com.

Endnotes

Chapter 1

Epigraph: Baltasar Gracián, *The Art of Worldly Wisdom*, trans. Joseph Jacobs (London: Macmillan, 1982).

1   Charles Darwin, *The Expression of the Emotions in Man and Animals* (New York: Oxford University Press, 1998); Robert Plutchik, *Emotions and Life: Perspectives from Psychology, Biology, and Evolution* (Washington, DC: American Psychological Association, 2003); Paul Ekman, *Emotions Revealed: Recognizing Faces and Feelings to Improve Communication and Emotional Life* (New York: Owl Books, 2003).

2   Raymond Chip Tafrate, Howard Kassinove, and Louis Dundin, "Anger Episodes in High and Low Trait Anger Community Adults," *Journal of Clinical Psychology* 58 (2002), 1573–90.

3   John Archer, "Sex Differences in Aggression between Heterosexual Partners: A Meta-analytic Review," *Psychological Bulletin* 126 (2000), 651–80.

Chapter 2

Epigraph: Lu Xun, *Essays* (San Francisco: New China Press, 1921), cited by Simon Leys (pseud. Pierre Ryckmans), *The Burning Forest: Essays on Chinese Culture and Politics* (New York: Holt, Rinehart and Winston, 1986).

4   See, for example, H. Kassinove, D. G. Sukhodolsky, S. V. Tsytsarev, and S. Solovyova, "Self-Reported Constructions of Anger Episodes in Russia and America," *Journal of Social Behavior and Personality* 12 (1997), 301–24; Raymond Chip Tafrate, Howard Kassinove, and Louis Dundin, "Anger Episodes in High and Low Trait Anger Community Adults," *Journal of Clinical Psychology* 58 (2002), 1573–90.

5   Albert Ellis, *Reason and Emotion in Psychotherapy*, rev. ed. (New York: Carol Publishing, 1994); Aaron T. Beck, *Prisoners of Hate: The Cognitive Basis of Anger, Hostility, and Violence* (New York: HarperCollins, 1999).

Chapter 3

Epigraph: Aldous Huxley, quoted in "Sayings of the Week," *The Observer*, 2 July 1961.

6   See, for example, B. J. Bushman, "Does Venting Anger Feed or Extinguish the Flame? Catharsis, Rumination, Distraction, Anger, and Aggressive Responding," *Journal of Personality and Social Psychology* 28 (2002), 724–31.

Chapter 4

Epigraph: John Steinbeck, *Sweet Thursday* (New York: Viking, 1954).

7   W. Wenqi, G. Jackson, A. D. Lu, H. W. Galinsky, S. D. Gosling, et al., "Regional Ambient Temperature Is Associated with Human Personality," *Nature Human Behaviour* 1 (2017), 890–95.

8   J. L. Deffenbacher, "Evidence for Effective Treatment of Anger-Related Disorders," in E. L. Feindler (ed.), *Anger-Related Disorders: A Practitioner's Guide to Comparative Treatments* (New York: Springer, 2006).

9   "Excessive Sleepiness: How Much Sleep Do We Really Need," National Sleep Foundation, accessed 17 June 2018, https://sleepfoundation.org/excessivesleepiness /content/how-much-sleep-do-we-really-need-0.

10   Lydia Saad, "The '40-Hour' Workweek Is Actually Longer—by Seven Hours," Gallup, 29 August 2014, http://news.gallup.com/poll/175286/hour-workweek -actually-longer-seven-hours.aspx.

11   See "Work Schedules: Shift Work and Long Hours" (video), Centers for Disease Control and Prevention, accessed 9 June 2018, https://www.cdc.gov/niosh/topics /workschedules/default.html. See also "Average Annual Hours Actually Worked," OECD iLibrary, accessed 9 June 2018, https://www.oecd-ilibrary.org/employment /data/hours-worked/average-annual-hours-actually-worked_data-00303-en.

12   M. D. van der Zwaag, S. Fairclough, E. Spiridon, and J. H. D. M. Westerink, "The Impact of Music on Affect during Anger-Inducing Drives," in S. D'Mello, A. Graesser, B. Schuller, and J. C. Martin (eds.), *Affective Computing and Intelligent Interaction* (Berlin and Heidelberg: Springer, 2011).

13   W. Pieschl and S. Fegers, "Violent Lyrics = Aggressive Listeners?," *Journal of Media Psychology* 28 (2016), 32–41.

14   See M. Bensimon, T. Einat, and A. Gilboa, "The Impact of Relaxing Music on Prisoners' Levels of Anxiety and Anger," *International Journal of Offender Therapy and Comparative Criminology* 59 (2015), 406–23; Seyedah Maryam Fakhrhosseini, Steven Landry, Yin Yin Tan, Saru Bhattarai, and Myounghoon Jeon, "If You're Angry, Turn the Music On: Music Can Mitigate Anger Effects on Driving Performance," in Shamsi Iqbal, Erika Miller, and Yuqing Wu (eds.), *Proceedings of the 6th International Conference on Automotive User Interfaces and Interactive Vehicular Applications* (New York: ACM Publications, 2014).

15   J. Haviland-Jones, J. J. Rosario, P. W. Wilson, and T. McGuire, "An Environmental Approach to Positive Emotion: Flowers," *Evolutionary Psychology* 3 (2005), 104–32.

16   H. Wohlfarth, "The Effects of Color-Psychodynamic Environmental Color and Lighting Modification of Elementary Schools on Blood Pressure and Mood: A Controlled Study," *International Journal of Biosocial Research* 7:1 (1985), 9–16; Lindsey Gruson, "Color Has a Powerful Effect on Behavior, Researchers Assert," *New York Times*, 19 October 1982, https://www.nytimes.com/1982/10/19/science /color-has-a-powerful-effect-on-behavior-researchers-assert.html.

17   N. Nadkarni, L. Schnacker, P. Hasbach, T. Thys, and E. Crockett, "From Orange to Blue: How Nature Imagery Affects Inmates in the Blue Room," *Corrections Today* (January–February 2017), 36–40.

18   E. Spiridon and S. H. Fairclough, "The Effects of Ambient Blue Light on Anger Levels: Applications in the Design of Unmanned Aircraft GCS," *International Journal of Unmanned Systems Engineering* 5:3 (2017), 53–69.

Chapter 5

Epigraph: Charles Adams, *The Life of Samuel Johnson* (New York: Carlton & Lanahan, 1969).

Chapter 6

Epigraph: Dennis Gabor, *Inventing the Future* (New York: Knopf, 1964).

19   See E. C. Chang, T. J. D'Zurilla, and L. J. Sanna, eds, *Social Problem Solving: Theory, Research, and Training* (Washington, DC: American Psychological Association, 2004).

Chapter 7

Epigraph: Alphonse Karr, *Lettres écrites de mon jardin* (Paris: Michel Lévy Frères, 1853).

20   Albert Ellis, *Reason and Emotion in Psychotherapy*, rev. ed. (New York: Carol Publishing, 1994); Aaron T. Beck, *Prisoners of Hate: The Cognitive Basis of Anger, Hostility, and Violence* (New York: HarperCollins, 1999).

Chapter 8

Epigraph: John Ruskin, *The Crown of Wild Olive* (New York: Wiley, 1978).

Chapter 9

Epigraph: Thomas Szasz, *The Second Sin* (Garden City, NY: Anchor Press, 1973).

21   See "Story Topic: Reconciliation," The Forgiveness Project, 2018, http://theforgivenessproject.com/topics/reconciliation/.

22   David R. Blumenthal, "Repentance and Forgiveness," *Cross Currents*, accessed 24 June 2018, http://www.crosscurrents.org/blumenthal.htm.

23   Zeinab, "Islam Teaches Us to Be Forgiving and Pardoning," Islamic Forum, 25 January 2005, https://www.gawaher.com/topic/7231-islam-teaches-us -to-be-forgiving-and-pardoning/.

24   See "Father of Murdered Pizza Delivery Driver Forgives Killer, Brings Court to Tears," 8 November 2017, https://www.youtube.com/watch?v=rS1rFr9KOAc.

25   An interview with this father can be found in Raymond Chip Tafrate and Howard Kassinove, *Anger Management in Counseling and Psychotherapy* (video), distributed by Psychotherapy.net.

26   Primo Levi, *Survival in Auschwitz: The Nazi Assault on Humanity*, trans. Stuart Woolf (New York: Collier, 1993).

27   Viktor Frankl, *Man's Search for Meaning* (Boston: Beacon Press, 1959).

28   See Carl Schreck, " 'I Was No Longer a Child': Auschwitz Survivor Eva Mozes Kor," *Radio Free Europe/Radio Liberty*, 25 January 2015, https://www.rferl.org/a/auschwitz-survivor-eva-mozes-kor/26812368.html.

Chapter 10

Epigraph: Bill Steigerwald, "Lofty Ideals" (interview with Sir Edmund Hillary), *Pittsburgh Post-Gazette*, 9 November 1998.

29   See Herbert Benson and Miriam Z. Klipper, *The Relaxation Response* (New York: Harper Paperbacks, 2000).

Chapter 11

Epigraph: Benjamin Brewster, *Yale Literary Magazine*, February 1882.

Chapter 12

Epigraph: William H. Whyte, "Is Anybody Listening?," *Fortune* magazine, 1950.

30   Key to figure 12.1: (*top row, left to right*) angry, surprised, neutral; (*bottom row, left to right*) sad, angry, happy.

Chapter 13

Epigraph: Hara Estroff Marano, "Assertive, Not Aggressive," *Psychology Today*, 9 June 2016.

31   See Robert Alberti and Michael Emmons, *Your Perfect Right: Assertiveness and Equality in Your Life and Relationships*, 10th ed. (Oakland: Impact, 2017).

Raymond Chip Tafrate, PhD, is a clinical psychologist and professor in the criminology and criminal justice department at Central Connecticut State University. He is a fellow and supervisor at the Albert Ellis Institute in New York City, NY, and a member of the Motivational Interviewing Network of Trainers. He frequently consults with criminal justice agencies and programs regarding difficult-to-change problems such as anger dysregulation and criminal behavior. He has coauthored numerous books, and has presented his research throughout North America, Europe, Asia, and Australia.

Howard Kassinove, PhD, ABPP, is a board-certified clinical psychologist, former chairperson of the psychology department at Hofstra University, and past director of their PhD program in clinical and school psychology. Kassinove is a fellow of the American Psychological Association, the American Psychological Society, the Albert Ellis Institute, and the Behavior Therapy and Research Society. The editor of *Anger Disorders*, he has published more than sixty papers, and has lectured widely in the United States, Europe, and Asia.

Foreword writer **Matthew McKay, PhD**, is a professor at the Wright Institute in Berkeley, CA. He has authored and coauthored numerous books, including *The Relaxation and Stress Reduction Workbook*, *Self-Esteem*, *Thoughts and Feelings*, and more. McKay received his PhD in clinical psychology from the California School of Professional Psychology, and specializes in the cognitive behavioral treatment of anxiety and depression. He lives and works in the greater San Francisco Bay Area.

MORE BOOKS *from*
NEW HARBINGER PUBLICATIONS

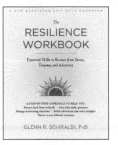

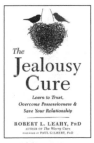

Register your **new harbinger** titles for additional benefits!

When you register your **new harbinger** title—purchased in any format, from any source—you get access to benefits like the following:

- Downloadable accessories like printable worksheets and extra content

- Instructional videos and audio files

- Information about updates, corrections, and new editions

Not every title has accessories, but we're adding new material all the time.

Access free accessories in 3 easy steps:

1. Sign in at NewHarbinger.com (or **register** to create an account).

2. Click on **register a book**. Search for your title and click the **register** button when it appears.

3. Click on the **book cover or title** to go to its details page. Click on **accessories** to view and access files.

That's all there is to it!

If you need help, visit:

NewHarbinger.com/accessories